THE PERFECT WOMAN

by

WALLACE GEOFFREY
and BASIL MITCHELL

LONDON
SAMUEL FRENCH LIMITED

Copyright © 1950 by Samuel French Ltd
All Rights Reserved

THE PERFECT WOMAN is fully protected under the copyright laws of the British Commonwealth, including Canada, the United States of America, and all other countries of the Copyright Union. All rights, including professional and amateur stage productions, recitation, lecturing, public reading, motion picture, radio broadcasting, television and the rights of translation into foreign languages are strictly reserved.

ISBN 978-0-573-12217-0

www.samuelfrench.co.uk

www.samuelfrench.com

For Amateur Production Enquiries

United Kingdom and World excluding North America

plays@SamuelFrench-London.co.uk

020 7255 4302/01

Each title is subject to availability from Samuel French,

depending upon country of performance.

CAUTION: Professional and amateur producers are hereby warned that THE PERFECT WOMAN is subject to a licensing fee. Publication of this play does not imply availability for performance. Both amateurs and professionals considering a production are strongly advised to apply to the appropriate agent before starting rehearsals, advertising, or booking a theatre. A licensing fee must be paid whether the title is presented for charity or gain and whether or not admission is charged.

The professional rights in this play are controlled by Samuel French Ltd, 52 Fitzroy Street, London, W1T 5JR.

No one shall make any changes in this title for the purpose of production. No part of this book may be reproduced, stored in a retrieval system, or transmitted in any form, by any means, now known or yet to be invented, including mechanical, electronic, photocopying, recording, videotaping, or otherwise, without the prior written permission of the publisher. No one shall upload this title, or part of this title, to any social media websites.

The right of Wallace Geoffrey and Basil Mitchell to be identified as author of this work has been asserted in accordance with Section 77 of the Copyright, Designs and Patents Act 1988.

THE PERFECT WOMAN

Produced at the Playhouse Theatre, London, on September 11th, 1948, with the following cast of characters:

(in the order of their appearance)

JOAN MERRIFIELD (Belmon's niece)	*Honor Shepherd*
GRUBB (The butler)	*Owen Fellowes*
PROFESSOR ARCHIBALD BELMON	*John Deverell*
DR JACKSON	*Peter Cozens*
BUDDY RAYMON	*Gordon Craig*
FREDDIE CAVENDISH	*Sonnie Hale*
ALBERT RAMSHEAD (Freddie's manservant)	*Charles Heslop*
FARINI (The Maitre d'hotel)	*Fred Berger*
WINKEL (a waiter)	*David Hurst*
LADY GEVIPHIE—pronounced " Goofy " (Freddie's Aunt)	*Ellen Pollock*
" ERMYNTRUDE " (The Robot)	

SYNOPSIS OF SCENES

ACT I

Professor Belmon's Library at " The Laurels ", on the outskirts of London. Seven p.m.

ACT II

A bedroom in a London hotel. Eight-thirty p.m.

ACT III

The same at Act II. Ten p.m.

[To face page 1 "The Perfect Woman"]

THE PERFECT WOMAN

ACT I

SCENE.—*The library of* PROFESSOR BELMON'S *house " The Laurels," on the outskirts of London. Seven p.m.*

The room, with stone-coloured walls, is a pleasant one, and is tastefully furnished and decorated. Up C. *two pillars flank an alcove, in the back wall of which there is a glass-panelled door leading to the laboratory. There are heavily curtained windows* R. *and* L. *of the door. The alcove leads off* R. *to the butler's quarters and kitchen, and a door* L. *of the alcove leads to the main front door. A low staircase of three steps runs off* R. *through an arch to the other rooms in the house. The fireplace, facing the audience, is* L. *A large comfortable sofa stands* R.C., *with an easy chair to match facing up* C. *below the fireplace. There is a writing desk, with an upright chair to it, against the wall up* R. *Below the staircase there is a carved oak chest with a bright cushion on it. An armchair stands below the desk, and two upright chairs* R. *and* L. *of the door up* C. *The well-filled bookcase stands against the wall down* L. *There is a small table with a telephone on it, and a small armchair* R. *of it, standing* L.C. *Another small table* R. *of the fireplace has a tray on it, with a decanter of whisky and a syphon of soda. The room is lit by a standard lamp up* R., *a table lamp on the table* R. *of the fireplace, the desk lamp, and wall brackets above the mantelpiece, in the arch over the stairs, and on the wall* R. *The floor and stairs are comfortably carpeted. A few pictures and ornaments complete the furnishing of the room. When the door to the laboratory up* C. *is opened, a glimpse is obtained of the chrome-legged stools and table on which are various bottles of chemicals, etc.*

(See the Ground Plan at the end of the Play.)

When the CURTAIN *rises, the stage is empty. A glow of light comes from the closed laboratory door up* C. *The only other light in the room is from the table lamp* R. *of the fireplace and the wall bracket in the arch over the stairs. After a moment,* JOAN MERRIFIELD, *aged about twenty-two, and wearing a negligee, enters stealthily* R., *descends the stairs, crosses, sits in the armchair* R. *of the table* L.C., *lifts the telephone receiver and dials a number. As she listens for the reply,* GRUBB *enters up* R., *sees* JOAN *and crosses quietly to* R. *of her.*

GRUBB. Can I help, miss?
JOAN (*turning, startled*). Oh, Grubb, never do that again.
GRUBB. Sorry, miss. Is there anything afoot?
JOAN. Definitely—some dirty work.
GRUBB. Am I in it, miss?
JOAN. Up to the neck.
GRUBB (*moving to the light switches* R. *of the fireplace*). Oh dear. (*From the wall switches, he switches on the standard lamp, the desk lamp, the wall brackets over the mantelpiece and the bracket on the wall up* R.) Might I suggest, miss, that you leave me out of one of your escapades?
JOAN. Ridiculous, Grubb, what would you do without a bit of excitement?
GRUBB (*moving above the sofa*). Maybe live a little longer, miss. (*He tidies the cushions on the sofa.*)
JOAN. A short life and a gay one is our motto.
GRUBB. Is it, miss? (*He empties the ashtray from the desk into the waste-paper basket.*)
JOAN. Certainly, but I don't want to spend most of it on this phone. (*Into the telephone.*) Hello.
GRUBB (*moving below the sofa*). What do you want, miss?
JOAN. I want to make certain my dress has been sent for tonight.
GRUBB. You're not going out, miss?
JOAN. Aren't I?
GRUBB. The Professor wouldn't like it, miss.
JOAN. All professors like—are bad smells. I'm fed up with being just a chemical formula to be kept in a cool place under control.
GRUBB. Quite, miss. Your uncle should know that certain chemicals confined in too small an area are apt to explode.
JOAN. You've said it, Grubb. Look out for a large bang. (*Into the telephone.*) Hello . . . Oh, at last. This is Miss Merrifield speaking—have you sent it yet? . . . The yellow one . . . What? Only white in stock? Who are you? . . . Sanitary engineers? Oh!
GRUBB (*moving up* C.). Cut off, miss, before they send you something.
JOAN (*replacing the receiver*). I'm sure that's the right number.

(PROFESSOR BELMON *and* DR JACKSON *are heard laughing off up* C.)

GRUBB. I shouldn't try again, miss. Your uncle and Dr Jackson are in the laboratory.
JOAN (*rising and moving to* GRUBB). Grubby, will you help me out?
GRUBB. And in, miss?
JOAN. As usual.
GRUBB. Oh, miss.
JOAN. You wouldn't let a pal down.
GRUBB. Never, miss.

ACT I] THE PERFECT WOMAN 3

JOAN. Bless you—and you'll lie a little if necessary?
GRUBB. Like a Member of Parliament, miss. Where will it be tonight, miss, the pantry or the coal hole?
JOAN. Oh, the pantry I think, and mind, not a word to uncle and Dr Jackson.
GRUBB. Look out, miss, here they come.

(*He exits up* R. JOAN *turns, runs to the stairs, and exits quickly* R. PROFESSOR ARCHIBALD BELMON *and* DR JACKSON *enter up* C.)

JACKSON (*as he enters*). You're too modest, my dear Professor. (*He moves down* R.) Until you showed her to me last night I wouldn't have believed it possible.

(BELMON *switches off the laboratory light, moves to the table* R. *of the fireplace, and proceeds to pour out two drinks.*)

As a doctor and scientist, I think that technically it's a great achievement.
BELMON. Thank you. I must say I'm rather proud of her myself. It's been a long job, you know. More than five years I've been working on it, and of course there's still room for improvement. (*He moves* C. *with the two drinks.*)
JACKSON (*moving* R. *of* BELMON). I suppose so, though it appears very nearly perfect to me. (*He takes one of the drinks from* BELMON.) Thanks. The movement is so easy and the balance is perfect.

(*The front door bell rings.*)

BELMON. That is achieved by a number of gyroscopes electrically driven.
JACKSON. Oh, I see. I suppose you'll present it at the Scientific Society's annual meeting next month?

(GRUBB *enters up* R., *crosses the alcove and exits up* L.)

BELMON. I intend to do so, but first I must have it thoroughly tested. All previous robots have been so unsatisfactory that the mere mention of the subject is received with suspicion and scepticism. In fact, a great number of people don't even know what a robot is.

(GRUBB *enters up* L.)

GRUBB. Beg pardon, sir. There's a person wishes to see you.
BELMON. What name?
GRUBB. He wouldn't give a name, sir—just said he'd come in answer to the advertisement, sir.
BELMON. Ah—the advertisement. Show him in, Grubb.
GRUBB. Just as you wish, sir.

(*He exits up* L.)

JACKSON (*handing his empty glass to* BELMON). Grubb doesn't seem to approve of your visitor. (*He moves and sits on the sofa at the* R. *end of it.*)

BELMON (*moving to the table* R. *of the fireplace*). He's not asked to. Now this is part of my scheme for introducing my robot woman to the world. (*He places the two empty glasses on the table.*) But before mentioning her to the Scientific Society, I want to have the report from an independent witness that she is indistinguishable from a real woman. (*He takes the box of cigarettes from the table, moves and offers a cigarette to* JACKSON.)

(JACKSON *shakes his head, takes his pipe, tobacco pouch and matches from his pocket, and proceeds to fill his pipe.*)

So I have advertised for a man who is willing to take her about London for a week— (*he eases* L.) and at the end of that time to bring her back to me.

JACKSON. Oh, I see. What a very good idea.

(GRUBB, *followed by* BUDDY RAYMON, *enters up* L.)

GRUBB (*announcing*). The answer to the advertisement, sir.

BUDDY (*to* GRUBB). Ta, Lofty. (*He moves* C.) Good evening, gentlemen.

(GRUBB *exits up* R.)

I presume that one or both of you is or are responsible for this advertisement. (*He reads from the newspaper he is carrying.*) " Wanted. Young man of refinement— " (*he clicks his tongue*) " in search of adventure, to place himself at disposal of advertisers for one week. Generous remuneration. Apply . . . "

BELMON. Yes, yes. That is my advertisement. I am seeking . . .

BUDDY. Pardon me, sir. You *were* seeking. Your search is ended. I, sir, am the man you want. The name's Buddy Raymon (*he shakes hands with* BELMON) and I come from Lambeth. (*He moves below the sofa.*) Though I'm well known in the West End, too. (*He offers his hand to* JACKSON *but withdraws it quickly. To* JACKSON.) Hard luck, chum. (*He turns to* BELMON.) In fact, sir, I'm so well known there ain't a town in this country where local prejudice don't make my existence, in a free and natural state, first cousin to an impossibility. For that reason I'm starting afresh, but I can't get going. Now your racket, sir, is just about my handwriting. (*He moves to* BELMON.) Adventure, that's what I'm after. (*He takes a cigarette from the still open box in* BELMON's *hand.*) Ay ay. Ta, tosh. (*He moves to the sofa, sits on it,* L. *of* JACKSON, *crosses his legs, displaying his brilliant socks.*) Now I got you all set. You're a couple of blokes that's got the racket all figured out, but you ain't got the guts to carry it through. Right ? (*He slaps* JACKSON *hard on the knee.*) I am the guts. Anything from a kidnapping to a slashing, it's all the same to me. Now then, spill it, and let's see where I figure on the payroll. (*He takes out his lighter, lights his cigarette, and sprawls comfortably on the sofa.*)

BELMON (*putting the cigarette box on the table* L.C.). Yes, but this particular undertaking is of such a delicate nature . . .

BUDDY. Then it's a good thing I called. Delicacy, sir, is my middle name. (*He wipes his nose on his sleeve.*) I got the touch— used to flog the fruit, see? Now, give us the gen, and I'm on.

BELMON. Yes, yes. But what I mean is—this is a matter where secrecy is essential.

BUDDY. Secrecy? That's what I'm noted for. Nobody ever heard me talk.

BELMON. Quite, quite. But as I was going to say, I should have to see your credentials before . . .

BUDDY (*to* JACKSON). Credentials, 'ark at 'im. (*To* BELMON.) Nobody can't show more than me, mate. I'm covered in 'em. Three broken ribs, and four broken bottle scars. 'Ere, don't take my word for it. 'Ave a butcher's at this. (*He rises and lowers his head for* BELMON *to see.*)

BELMON. No, no. That's quite unnecessary.

JACKSON (*rising and leading* BUDDY *down* R.). Look, I'm afraid you don't understand. My friend merely wants someone to escort a lady . . .

BUDDY. A lady. Well, look at that. Dead lucky thing for you I saw that advertisement. There ain't one in a million could fill the bill the way I can. You see, I got a way with the ladies. (*He takes a cellophane packet, containing a pair of Nylon stockings, from his pocket.*) 'Ere, screw. Nylons. Red 'ot, eh?

BELMON. Yes, but this is not an ordinary lady.

BUDDY (*replacing the packet in his pocket*). Well, well, well. You naughty old man you. (*To* JACKSON.) At his age an' all. Wha' a boy.

BELMON. No, no. You don't understand. I am looking for someone to take her about for a week. To theatres, hotels, race meetings.

BUDDY (*moving* C.). I got you. She's working the racket, and you merely want a bodyguard to lay off interference. I just step out of the picture and do everything she says. Right?

BELMON. On the contrary. She will do everything that you say.

(JACKSON *moves to the sofa and sits on it.*)

BUDDY. You bet she will, boy. I know 'ow to 'andle a doll like that.

BELMON. Well, yes, she is a sort of doll, but not the ordinary . . .

BUDDY (*moving* L. *of* JACKSON). I know the kind. I've seen thousands of 'em.

BELMON. I'm quite sure you haven't. This one is unique.

BUDDY. Foreign, eh? Well, it don't make no difference. I'll handle her. And my, if anybody tries to queer her I'll be right there on the job. D'you know what, (*to* JACKSON) two razors is the least I ever carry, and I'm red hot with both hands. (*He raises his knee sharply and demonstrates a butt with his head.*)

BELMON. But you don't understand.

JACKSON (*rising to* R. *of* BUDDY). I'm sorry, Mr Raymon. I'm afraid your talents would be wasted on this enterprise. It would be too tame for you.

BUDDY. I like it tame, and if it ain't tame enough, boy, I do the taming. (*He slaps* JACKSON'S *chest with the back of his right hand.*) Now then, where is the doll?

BELMON. At this moment she is in my laboratory.

BUDDY. In the where? Well, it don't matter where she is, I'll soon have her out of it.

BELMON (*moving to the door up* C.). Perhaps it will be better if you saw her first. (*He opens the door and switches on the light in the laboratory.*) Then you will understand.

BUDDY. Now you're talking. Fetch out the dame and you'll see. If she don't choose me for her escort first thing she sees me, then insult me, call me a working man.

BELMON. Well, will you come this way, please.

BUDDY (*moving up* C.). I'm right after you, cock. Right there, boy.

(BELMON *and* BUDDY *exit up* C. JACKSON *moves up* C. *As he does so,* JOAN *enters* R., *descends the stairs, crosses, sits in the armchair* R. *of the table* L.C., *lifts the telephone receiver and dials a number.*)

JACKSON. Hullo, Joan.

JOAN (*startled*). Oh, Dr Jackson. I didn't know anyone was here. I thought you were going out with Uncle Archie.

JACKSON. Yes, I am, but your uncle has a visitor. (*He moves to the sofa and sits on it.*) They're both in the laboratory.

JOAN. Oh, good. I really must telephone.

(BELMON *enters up* C., *closing the door behind him.*)

BELMON (*moving above the sofa*). I'm so sorry, my dear fellow. Why didn't you come with us?

(JACKSON *indicates* JOAN.)

(*He turns to* JOAN.) Joan, what are you doing here? You can't run about the house like that.

(*There are crashes and noises off up* C. BUDDY *enters hurriedly up* C.)

BUDDY (*as he enters*). Nark it. Nark it.

(JOAN *replaces the receiver, rises, runs across to the stairs and exits hurriedly* R.)

(*He moves down* C.) I'm not standing that from you or no one else.

BELMON. Whatever happened?

BUDDY. What happened? She just flew off the handle at me.

Anybody would have thought I'd just slashed her one and only boy friend. She was that mad.

BELMON (*moving up* C.). I do hope you haven't hurt her. (*He calls off up* C.) Stop.

(*The noises off up* C. *cease.* BELMON *switches off the laboratory light, closes the door and moves* R. *of* BUDDY.)

BUDDY. Hurt her. A bloke would need a battery of bren guns to hurt her. I've seen a few in my time but she comes across anything I've ever seen.

BELMON. That's all right, she's quiet now. Are you hurt?

BUDDY (*feeling his bones*). Well, my feelings is hurt. (*He sits in the armchair* L.C.) I've never had a dame fly out at me that way before.

BELMON. What did you do to cause her to do that?

BUDDY. Do? Nothing. I just go in there all dead polite like, and I say I'd love to have the pleasure . . .

BELMON (*moving* L. *of the sofa*). Ah! Love. Did you mention the word love?

BUDDY. Well, of course I did. I was only trying to be a bit la-di-da.

BELMON. I was going to warn you. When I made her I had to provide for every emergency, and in case any man should try and make love to her I arranged that the word love—should cause her to become so violent that no man would be likely to repeat the experiment.

BUDDY. What, make love to that creature?

BELMON. It's really for man's own protection. I know what it is to be disappointed in love myself. So I wanted to protect others, by nipping the sentiment in the bud.

BUDDY. Well, if anyone makes love to that thing, he deserves all he gets. I never saw such a cast iron . . .

BELMON. Well, in the ordinary way she's placid enough. (*He moves up* C.) Now, if you will come back with me . . .

BUDDY (*rising*). Come back. Not on your life. The job's off. You've had it. If I knew this place was nuthouse, I wouldn't have come anywhere near.

BELMON. It's all right, it's all right. I shall have to find someone else. (*He presses the bell-push* R. *of the door up* C.)

BUDDY (*moving* L. *of* BELMON). Find someone else? Well, I wish him joy.

BELMON. Quite, quite. Well, there's no harm done.

BUDDY. Harm? If I did my duty as a citizen, I'd report the whole thing to the police—but lucky for you that ain't my way.

BELMON. Well, I'm quite sure you wouldn't do that, sir.

(GRUBB *enters up* R.)

GRUBB. You rang, sir?

BUDDY. Rang? Rang nothing.

(He turns and exits quickly up L.)

BELMON. Good evening. Show the gentleman the door, Grubb.
(The front door is heard to slam off up L.)
GRUBB. He seems to have found it, sir.
BELMON. Well, see he keeps on the right side of it.
GRUBB. Very good, sir.
(He crosses BELMON *and exits up* L.)
JACKSON. I think you may congratulate yourself, my dear fellow.
BELMON *(moving down* C.). Yes, I think so.
(JOAN *enters* R. *and descends the stairs.*)
JOAN. Uncle.
BELMON. Joan, go and get dressed at once.
JOAN *(moving* R. *of* BELMON). Uncle, who was that man?
BELMON. A business friend.
JOAN. But who was the lady who frightened him?
BELMON. What?
JOAN. The lady in there.
JACKSON. It's only a machine, Joan.
BELMON. Yes, dear, it's something I've invented. He just didn't know how to work it.
JOAN. But he called it she.
JACKSON. Men often call machinery she.
BELMON. Of course they do, it's short for machine. Now look here, Joan, you go up to your room at once.
JOAN. Can I telephone first?
BELMON. What for?
JOAN. I'm going to the theatre.
BELMON. Who with?
JOAN. Alone.
BELMON. Certainly not.
JOAN. But it's a new play, the first night.
BELMON. I'll take you tomorrow.
JOAN. It may not be on tomorrow.
BELMON. Now, Joan, promise me that you won't go out alone tonight.
JOAN. All right, Uncle—I promise you that I won't go out alone.
BELMON. That's a good girl. Stay in and read a good book. I'll lend you my " *Uncle Tom's Cabin*". Come along, Jackson, I want to show you those blue-prints for that other invention of mine.

(JACKSON *rises and exits with* BELMON *up* R. JOAN *eases* L.C. *and stands sullenly and indecisively looking at the telephone.* GRUBB *carrying a large dress box, enters up* L.)

GRUBB. It's here, miss.
JOAN. Oh! It's no use, Grubb, he won't let me go alone. I must have an escort. Can you help me, Grubb?

ACT I]   THE PERFECT WOMAN   9

GRUBB. No, I'm sorry, miss, it's not my night out.
JOAN.   Oh, do be serious, Grubb. I'd do anything to get out tonight.
GRUBB. Careful, miss, that's a dangerous mood.

(*The front door bell rings.*)

Ah! The advertisement again, I presume.
JOAN. Advertisement?
GRUBB. Don't you think you'd better go to your room, miss, it may be someone for the master.
JOAN (*taking the box from* GRUBB). Oh, I forgot. You have no right to talk to me when I'm not dressed, Grubb. You have no delicacy at all.
GRUBB. Sorry, miss.

(*He exits up* L. JOAN *stands for a moment undecided where she shall go, then exits up* R., *taking the dress box with her.*)

(*Off.*) Come this way, sir.

(FREDDIE CAVENDISH, *followed by* GRUBB *and* ALBERT "BABA" RAMSHEAD, *enters up* L. BABA *carries hat, gloves and umbrella.* FREDDIE *eases* R. *of the armchair* L.C. *and hands the hat he carries to* GRUBB, *who moves* R. *of him.*)

BABA (*moving quickly* R. *of* GRUBB). Here, none of that. (*He snatches* FREDDIE'S *hat from* GRUBB.)
FREDDIE (*reaching in front of* GRUBB *and snatching his hat from* BABA). No, no. I gave it to him. (*He hands his hat again to* GRUBB.)

(BABA *gives his hat, gloves and umbrella to* GRUBB.)

GRUBB. If you will have the goodness to wait here a moment, sir, I will inform the Professor.
FREDDIE. The who?
GRUBB. The Professor, the master, sir.
FREDDIE. Oh, yes, the master.
BABA (*easing down* R.). The boss.
GRUBB. Did you wish just the one name, sir?
FREDDIE. The what?
GRUBB. You wish to announce just Mr Cavendish?
FREDDIE. Yes, just Mr Cavendish.
GRUBB. Just the one name.
FREDDIE. Well, you could mention Claude Charles Tregelles Frederick if you feel like it.
GRUBB. No, I meant, sir . . .
FREDDIE. You might make a combination of them. Why not try a treble of Claude Charles and Frederick?
BABA. Any to come all on Tregelles.
FREDDIE. Yes, double them up, make a good bet.

GRUBB. You misunderstand me, sir. I meant did your friend wish his name announced?
FREDDIE. Did he? When?
GRUBB. Now, sir.
FREDDIE. I'll ask him. (*He crosses to* L. *of* BABA.) Did you wish your name mentioned or not?
BABA. Not.
FREDDIE (*moving* R. *of* GRUBB). Not.
GRUBB. Yes, sir, Mr Nott, sir. (*He turns and moves up* C.)
FREDDIE. No, not Mr Nott. (*He crosses to* L.) Oh, Lord . . .
GRUBB (*stopping and turning*). Yes, sir. Lord Nott. Very good, sir.
FREDDIE. No, not Lord Nott, Mr Nott, or any Nott. Just not, that's all. (*To* BABA.) I say, would you deal with him? Not not not all the time. (*He moves down* L.)
BABA (*moving* L. *of the sofa*). Allow me, sir, allow me. (*To* GRUBB.) What the hell's the matter with you, my man? You get in there and tell your boss there are two gents waiting to see him. And be quick about it. Go on.
GRUBB. Yes, sir. Very good, sir.

(*He exits hurriedly up* R.)

FREDDIE (*moving to the table* L.C.). Ah, manna from heaven. (*He takes a cigarette from the box on the table.*) All right, Baba, but don't lose your temper. You'll raise your blood pressure.
BABA. No, sir, I won't. But did you ever hear the . . . Mr Nott, Lord Nott? One name or two? I never did in all . . .
FREDDIE (*moving above the sofa*). Yes, but he's only a butler, you know.
BABA (*moving to the table* R. *of the fireplace*). Well, I'm only a butler myself if it comes to that, but I trust I have more intelligence than that mutton-headed moron. Good God, what must his master be like? (*He proceeds to pour out two drinks.*)
FREDDIE (*lighting his cigarette*). Yes, well, don't judge a master by his butler. I'm sure my aunt wouldn't like to be judged by you. (*He picks up the ashtray from the desk and moves with it below the sofa.*)
BABA. Judged by me—I know what the sentence would be if she were. But don't forget, I'm not her butler any longer.
FREDDIE (*sitting on the sofa at the* R. *end of it*). Yes, I'm afraid that's my fault.
BABA. Oh, I'm not blaming you, sir. (*He moves to* FREDDIE *with the drinks.*) I blame her ladyship's entire lack of discrimination. (*He hands a drink to* FREDDIE.)
FREDDIE. Oh, welcome stranger.
BABA. Soda, sir? (*He imitates the hissing sound of a syphon.*)
FREDDIE. Don't drown it.
BABA. My best respects, sir.

ACT I]   THE PERFECT WOMAN   11

FREDDIE. To you.
BABA. *Ora pro nobis.* (*He drinks.*)
FREDDIE. Amen. (*He drinks.*)
BABA. No, very hard-hearted, her ladyship, sir, if I may say so, with all due respect. Very hard-hearted indeed.
FREDDIE. Definitely flinty. And a very bad judge of character.
BABA. A remarkably poor judge, sir.
FREDDIE. The very idea that you were leading me astray.
BABA. Ridiculous, sir, ridiculous. Me that has known you since you depended on a safety pin. No, sir, no. When she turned you out I knew where my duty lay—me leading you astray. A malicious misrepresentation of probabilities, sir.
FREDDIE. Quite. Good heavens, you couldn't lead a rabbit astray. (*He finishes his drink.*)
BABA. Well, I've never tried to actually, sir. I've never met a rabbit who needed leading in that direction. All the rabbits I have known have at a very early age . . .
FREDDIE (*interrupting*). All right, Baba.

(BABA *finishes his drink.*)

I don't think I want to hear your rural reminiscences, thank you. (*He hands his empty glass to* BABA.) But to return to my aunt.
BABA (*moving with the glasses to the table* R. *of the fireplace*). Oh, heaven forbid.
FREDDIE. I hope you don't bear her any malice, Baba.

(BABA *drains the glasses on to the carpet, rubs the whisky in with his foot, and cleans the glasses with his handkerchief.*)

BABA. No. No malice at all, sir. It's not that I mind getting the sack myself, but I cannot forgive her for the way she's treated you.
FREDDIE. Oh, don't think about it. (*He puts his feet up on the sofa, leans back and places the ashtray on his chest.*)
BABA (*pouring out two drinks*). Well, I'll try not to, sir. I'll try not to. Fancy cutting off your allowance at a moment's notice like that.
FREDDIE. Yes, that was rather a blow.
BABA. It's not good for a young man to have his allowance cut off.
FREDDIE. It's a very painful procedure, I might tell you.
BABA. Wasn't as if you'd done any harm either, sir.
FREDDIE. Well, I hadn't really, had I ?
BABA. No, sir, no. Just a boyish prank every now and then. Just a little innocent fun here and there.
FREDDIE. Personally, I thought it was very clever of me to select a tobacconist's daughter, with the shortage.
BABA (*moving to* FREDDIE *with the drinks*). She should have been very glad of your high spirits. (*He hands a drink to* FREDDIE.)

FREDDIE. My aunt has never been glad of anything I have ever done. She hates anything unconventional.
BABA. Yes, very unbohemian, sir.
FREDDIE. You've said it.
BABA. But she'll relent.
FREDDIE. D'you think so?
BABA. Oh, yes, sir. In time. She can't mean you to go without money for ever. (*He drinks, emptying his glass.*)
FREDDIE. Still, I must live. (*He drinks.*)
BABA. Yes, very unfortunate.
FREDDIE. What do you mean by that crack?
BABA (*moving to the table* R. *of the fireplace*). I mean it's unfortunate you can't live on nothing.
FREDDIE. But I don't want to live on nothing. I don't like nothing. It doesn't suit me.
BABA (*pouring himself another drink*). No, sir. It doesn't suit your creditors either. Would you care for another drink, sir?
FREDDIE. No, thank you.
BABA (*holding up the decanter*). We have plenty.
FREDDIE. No, no. (*He holds up his glass.*) Still got some—look.
BABA (*moving with his drink to the armchair* L.C.). Oh, I'm not alluding to myself, sir. Money doesn't worry me, luckily. (*He sits.*)
FREDDIE. Well, I can assure you none of my money'll worry you for a very long time.
BABA. Oh, that's all right, sir. I'm only too glad to serve the young master for nothing. I'm one of the old school, I am. Service without thought of self, faithful unto death—if necessary, of course.
FREDDIE. Yes, that all sounds very noble, Baba—but not very intelligent.

(GRUBB *enters up* R. FREDDIE *quickly conceals his glass under the sofa.* BABA *quickly conceals his drink behind the telephone receiver.*)

GRUBB. The Professor will be with you in a moment, sir. (*He sees* FREDDIE'S *feet on the sofa and moves below it.*)

(FREDDIE *raises his feet a few inches as* GRUBB *flicks the sofa under them, with his hand.* GRUBB *moves up* C., *turns and looks suspiciously around.*)

BABA. Anything missing?
GRUBB. No, sir.
BABA (*rising and moving* L. *of* GRUBB). Listen, Jeeves. If we wanted to pinch anything, we should go elsewhere where there was something to pinch. We shouldn't come here at all. Do you understand that? Go on—get out.
GRUBB (*almost speechless*). Yes, sir. Very good, sir.

(*He turns and exits up* R.)

FREDDIE. Very tactfully put, Baba.

BABA (*easing down* C.). I thought so. Fancy thinking we wanted to pinch something.
FREDDIE. Oh, I don't think he thought that.
BABA. I know what he thought, sir. His mind's an open book to me. I know these butlers. Pampered parasites.
FREDDIE. Look—will you shut up? You're going to get us thrown out of here before we're really settled in. I like this place. I like their hospitality. (*He retrieves his glass, drinks, and replaces the glass under the sofa.*)
BABA (*moving to the* L. *end of the sofa*). May I trouble you, sir?
FREDDIE (*removing his feet*). Certainly.
BABA (*sitting on the sofa,* L. *of* FREDDIE). I wonder what this job is?
FREDDIE (*sitting up*). Well, it may be something very exciting. (*He places the ashtray on the* R. *arm of the sofa.*) I thought that advertisement sounded very, very mysterious.
BABA. It certainly did, sir.
FREDDIE. It may be something political. Secret Service stuff. Dick Barton—that sort of thing.
BABA. What would that mean, sir?
FREDDIE. Oh, I don't know. Tied up, (*he puts his hand to his chin*) water up to here—can't get away, probably getting killed. You never know.
BABA. Killed? Both of us, do you think?
FREDDIE. Baba, you said you'd stand by me in this.
BABA. Yes indeed, sir, service without thought of self, sir. Faithful unto . . .
FREDDIE. Yes, all right, we've had that. You must try and forget that you're a servant.
BABA. I have practically forgotten it, sir.
FREDDIE. Well, relax, and don't call me sir.
BABA. Very good, sir. All right, sir. I won't, sir.
FREDDIE. Thank you, sir. (*He looks around.*) The old cock's a long time, isn't he?
BABA. Yes. Drink up and have another.

(FREDDIE *picks up his glass and drinks. As he does so, the voices of* BELMON *and* JACKSON *are heard off up* R. FREDDIE *hurriedly replaces the glass under the sofa.* BELMON *and* JACKSON *enter up* R. FREDDIE *and* BABA *rise.*)

BELMON (*moving down* C.). I'm sorry to have kept you waiting, Mr Cavendish.
FREDDIE. Not at all.
BABA. Not at all.
FREDDIE ⎱ (*singing together to the tune of* " *William Tell* "). Not at
BABA ⎰ all, not at all.
FREDDIE. Sorry, Professor, silly thing we do.

(JACKSON *eases* L. *of the sofa.*)

BELMON. You are Mr Cavendish?
FREDDIE. Yes, that's right, Cavendish.
BELMON. My name is Belmon, Professor Belmon. How do you do?
FREDDIE. How do you do? ⎫
BABA. How do you do? ⎬ *(They both bow.)*
BELMON. And this is my friend Dr Jackson, Mr Cavendish.
JACKSON. How do you do?
FREDDIE. How do you do? ⎫
BABA. How do you do? ⎬ *(They both bow.)*
BELMON. Dr Jackson is in my confidence.
FREDDIE. In where?
BELMON. In my confidence.
FREDDIE *(to* BABA*)*. Oh, they're in conference, we'd better go.
BABA. No, confidence.
FREDDIE. Oh, confidence. I'm sorry, Professor, it's the wrong ear.
BELMON. And you friend here—is he . . . ?
FREDDIE. Oh, he's in my confidence, too. Rather, splendid fellow. I'd like you to have met him—oh, of course you can, can't you? Professor Belmon, Dr Jackson, this is Baba.
JACKSON. How do you do? *(He bows.)*
BABA. How do you do? ⎫
FREDDIE. How do you do? ⎬ *(They both bow.)*
BELMON *(absent-mindedly ; to* JACKSON*)*. How do you do? How do you do, Mr Baba?
FREDDIE. No, no, you mustn't call him that.
BELMON. I beg your pardon.

(JACKSON *eases up* L.C.*, leans against the pillar, and proceeds to fill and light his pipe while listening to the ensuing conversation.*)

FREDDIE. No, his name is not Baba, his name's Ramshead.
BELMON. But I thought you said . . . ?
FREDDIE. No, I call him Baba, because of Ramshead—you know, ram, sheep, *(he bleats)* baaa-a.
BELMON. Oh, I see, a sort of nickname.
FREDDIE. Yes, that's right, Professor, a nickname. *(To* BABA.*)* Gets on to it quickly, doesn't he?
BELMON *(to* BABA*)*. And your real name is Ramshead?
BABA. No, no, it isn't. My real name is Ramsbottom, My father was a Ramsbottom. A very prominent citizen. But I changed it to Ramshead—for reasons that must be obvious to you.
BELMON. I'm afraid they're not. I mean, if your name is Rams-bottom, why change it?
BABA. Well, Ramsbottom's all right at home ; but it's not a name to make your way in the world with. So when I went into the world I became Ramshead.
FREDDIE. Yes, so as he'd get there sooner.

Baba. Mind you, there was nothing underhand about it.
Freddie. Oh, no. It's only going from one extreme to the other.
Belmon. Well, I suppose it's none of my business.
Freddie. No, it isn't really, it's between him and the ram.
Belmon. Well, gentlemen, I take it you've read my advertisement. (*He bows to* Freddie.) Is it your intention to enter jointly upon this enterprise?
Freddie (*bowing to* Belmon). My friend is indispensable to me.
Belmon. Well, will you sit down and I will explain my project to you. Would you like a drink?
Freddie (*sitting on the sofa*, R. *end*). ⎱ (*together*.) No more, thank
Baba (*sitting on the sofa*, L. *end*). ⎰ you.
Belmon. Well. (*He moves to the armchair* L.C. *and sits*.) Now, in the first place I have a surprising thing to tell you gentlemen. I have made a woman.
Freddie. You've what?
Belmon. I have made a woman.
Freddie. *You* have?
Belmon. Yes.
Freddie (*to* Baba). He's made a woman.
Belmon. Mind you, this is strictly in confidence.
Freddie (*to* Baba). Ah, it's in confidence.
Baba. Ah, that's how they do make them.
Belmon. Naturally, I'm very proud of this work, as I have done it entirely alone.

(Freddie *and* Baba *look knowingly at each other*.)

No other man has ever achieved such a thing; they've tried, but they couldn't do it.
Freddie. Exactly what have you—er—made her do?
Belmon. I can make her do anything—well, perhaps not everything, not all that I should like her to do; but undoubtedly she is the most perfect thing of her kind yet produced—really beautiful. But perhaps I shouldn't say " she ". Actually, she's of no sex.
Freddie. No sex?
Belmon. No sex.
Freddie. But there isn't a no sex.
Baba. You mean Middlesex.
Belmon. No, no, no. Don't you understand—she's a robot.
Freddie ⎱
Baba   ⎰ (*together*). Ohhh-h-h.
Freddie. She's a robot.
Belmon (*rising*). Perhaps I'd better show her to you. (*He crosses to* Jackson *and speaks to him*.)
Freddie. I wish you would. (*To* Baba.) What the devil's a robot?
Baba. Don't you know? Oh, robot—that's a polite way of pronouncing Rowbottom. Like Chumley.

FREDDIE. Oh, I see, or Marshbanks.

BELMON (*to* JACKSON). Possibly—I never thought of that. (*To* FREDDIE *and* BABA.) Gentlemen, I suppose you know what a robot is ?

FREDDIE. Oh, yes, my friend has just explained it to me. It's like Chumley.

BELMON. Splendid. Then perhaps you've had experience with robots before.

BABA. Yes, I once knew a family of Robots.

FREDDIE. Yes, there were big botts and little botts, you know.

BABA. Mark you—that was many years ago.

BELMON. Yes, but you'll find that my robot is quite different.

BABA. Oh, a different branch ?

BELMON. A different branch of science entirely. True, she has a somewhat mechanical figure.

BABA. Many of them have. Gay deceivers, they call them.

FREDDIE. Yes.

BELMON. But I am convinced that when the world knows of her, she will become famous, and make me famous too. (*He pauses.*) But before introducing her to the world, I must have her thoroughly tested.

FREDDIE. Tested ?

(JACKSON *turns to the table* R. *of the fireplace and proceeds to pour himself a drink. Unnoticed,* JOAN *peers round the corner up* R.)

BELMON. Tried out, and that is where you come in.

FREDDIE. I come in when she's tried out.

BELMON. Precisely. I want you to take charge of her for a week.

FREDDIE. Take charge of her, Professor ?

BELMON. Yes, take her everywhere, everywhere that you go.

FREDDIE. What—everywhere ?

BELMON. Well, everywhere that one could take a lady.

(JACKSON, *with his drink in his hand, eases to the fireplace.*)

FREDDIE. Yes, just what I was wondering.

BELMON. Take her to an hotel, book a double room and register her as your wife. Of course, you'll have to sleep in the same room, Mr Cavendish.

FREDDIE. Yes, they generally do, don't they ?

(JOAN *enters up* R. *with the dress box and exits unnoticed into the laboratory.*)

BELMON. Then you'll have to book a suite, because you must have all your meals in private ; you see, she can't eat. Then you'll have to order meals for two and eat everything yourself, so that no one will know she hasn't had any. Take her to the theatre, take her to the races. Take her about generally. She will do everything you tell her, but you must not ask her any questions, because she can't talk.

FREDDIE. Oh, she can't talk now.

BELMON. Then at the end of the week I want you to bring her back to me and tell me how you got on.

FREDDIE. Well, if she can't eat, and she can't talk, we should have got on very well I should think, Professor.

(JOAN *peers round the corner again, then quietly exits up* R.)

BELMON. I shall want your written and signed statement that no one has suspected her. Oh, by the way, (*he feels in his pockets*) I have here a list of key words to which she will react. Now, what have I done with it? What have I done with it? (*He crosses quickly above the sofa to the desk and looks on it for the lists.*)

JACKSON (*picking up the lists from the mantelpiece*). Here they are, Professor, on the mantelpiece.

(BELMON *hurriedly crosses below the sofa to* JACKSON. *As he does so,* FREDDIE *makes faces at* BELMON'S *back.*)

BABA (*to* FREDDIE). That's why the doctor's in the house.

FREDDIE (*tapping his forehead; to* BABA). Of course. Probably thinks he's a poached egg. Come on, let's go before they lock the doors.

(FREDDIE *and* BABA *rise.*)

BELMON (*turning*). Well, Mr Cavendish, before giving you these lists, what d'you think? Does this adventure appeal to you?

FREDDIE (*to* JACKSON). Doctor, we're going now, if you would like to attend to him.

JACKSON. Attend to him?

BELMON. But my dear sir, I'm asking you about this experiment of mine.

FREDDIE. Oh, we're still on that, are we? Oh, well, see you on visitors' day. We'll bring you some fruit.

BELMON. Oh, how silly of me. I never mentioned the financial side of it.

FREDDIE. No, you haven't, have you?

BELMON. I expect you would like to know.

FREDDIE. We would—rather.

(FREDDIE *and* BABA *sit on the sofa,* BABA L. *of* FREDDIE.)

BELMON. Of course, you will understand that as I want an unbiased report, it will be quite impossible to offer you a fee.

(FREDDIE *and* BABA *rise.*)

FREDDIE. Oh, thanks very much.

(FREDDIE *and* BABA *start to go.*)

BELMON. But I should of course, pay all expenses.

FREDDIE } (*together*). Oh.
BABA

BELMON. That would include your expenses and your friend's, and, of course, the woman's as well.

FREDDIE. Oh, the old fiddle-sheet.

(FREDDIE *and* BABA *resume their seats on the sofa*.)

BELMON. Then I think it would be quite legitimate to make you some compensation for the time you will be giving.

BABA. Oh, I think so, too. More than legitimate, legal in fact.

FREDDIE. Yes.

BELMON. I presume your time is of some value, Mr Cavendish.

FREDDIE. Of very great value, Professor. At the last—er—valuation I forget what it came to. What was it, Baba?

BABA. Forty shillings, or a month.

BELMON. One month? But I should only want you for one week.

BABA. Well, that makes it a little more expensive, what with purchase tax, one thing and another.

FREDDIE. Yes, you're halving the time and doubling the work, aren't you?

BELMON. I quite appreciate that, and I had thought that fifty pounds might meet the case. (*He turns to* JACKSON.)

FREDDIE. Fifty pounds.

BABA. That's real money that is.

FREDDIE. You bet it is real money. Oh, what a pity the whole scheme's screwy.

BABA. Well, even if it's imitation money we could always . . .

FREDDIE. Yes, we could, couldn't we. Wait a minute, is it legal to take money from a half-wit?

BABA. Of course it is, sir. That's how half the world gets it. Wait a minute. Don't jump at it, sir.

BELMON (*turning*). Well, Mr Cavendish, what do you think?

FREDDIE (*rising*). Well, Professor, (*he eases* C.) I've been discussing it with my friend here, who always acts as my manager in cases like this,

(BABA *lounges back on the sofa, with an important air.*)

and we rather thought . . .

BELMON. Not enough, eh?

FREDDIE. Well, you did say fifty pounds.

BELMON. I had suggested that, but of course, if you and your friend had thought of another figure yourselves . . .

(FREDDIE *turns to* BABA, *who makes indications with his hands to raise the price.*)

FREDDIE (*turning to* BELMON). Well, we had rather thought of—yes—fifty-one.

BELMON. Well, don't let a pound divide us.

FREDDIE. Oh, I'd hate a pound to do that.

BELMON. And, of course, there are two of you.

FREDDIE. Well, there are, aren't there?

BELMON. I want you to be satisfied.

ACT I] THE PERFECT WOMAN 19

FREDDIE. We'd like to be satisfied, too.
BELMON. Shall we say sixty pounds, then?
FREDDIE }
BABA   } *(together).* Sixty pounds.
BELMON. And say no more about it.
FREDDIE. And say no more about—what?
BABA. Wait a minute. (*He rises.*) We'll say no more about it after we've got the money.
BELMON. Exactly. I will send you a cheque as soon as the woman is safely returned to me. (*He sits in the armchair* L.C.)

(FREDDIE *and* BABA *look disappointed.*)

FREDDIE. Ah, he's brought his woman into it again.
BELMON. By the way, I expect you will want a little ready money for expenses—petty cash.
BABA. Not too petty.
BELMON (*taking his wallet from his pocket*). If I give you thirty pounds now——

(FREDDIE *nearly collapses.*)

—will that do to go on with? (*He proceeds to count out the notes.*)
FREDDIE. I could go quite a long way with that.
JACKSON. Perhaps you had better let the Professor know where you are, in case he wants to get in touch with you.
FREDDIE. Well, that rather depends on—er— (*to* BELMON) don't stop, (*to* JACKSON) on the woman, doesn't it?
BELMON. But my dear sir, I told you she can't speak. She will do anything you tell her, but she can't talk. You see, she is controlled entirely by radio waves.
FREDDIE. Of course she is.
BELMON. And there are key words for each action. For instance, you might say, "Will you sit down," or "Would you like to sit down," or "Come and sit down," and she will.
FREDDIE. Sit down.
BELMON. Precisely. As long as you use the key word "sit". (*He chuckles.*) No other robot has ever succeeded in doing that before. It makes it impossible to tell that she is not a human being.
FREDDIE. Not a what?
BELMON. Not a human being—not a real woman.
FREDDIE. But she is a real woman, isn't she?
BELMON. But my dear sir, I've been telling you all along, that it is a robot figure I have made.
FREDDIE (*looking at* JACKSON). Oh, oh of course it is,

(JACKSON *nods confirmation.*)

but I mean, she does look like a woman.
BELMON. Exactly. No one can tell the difference.

FREDDIE. No, they couldn't, could they ? (*He indicates the notes in* BELMON'S *hand.*) But I'm—er—interrupting you.
BELMON (*looking at the notes*). Oh, yes, yes. (*He turns to* JACKSON.) Jackson, could you lend me ten pounds ? I find I'm rather short.

(JACKSON *takes his wallet from his pocket, counts out ten one-pound notes and hands them to* BELMON.)

FREDDIE (*whispering excitedly to* BABA). It's not a real woman at all.
BABA. No, we're in.

(FREDDIE *and* BABA *make gestures of elation.*)

BELMON (*rising and crossing to* FREDDIE). Here are the thirty pounds, Mr Calveshead.

(FREDDIE *takes the notes and puts them in his pocket.*)

(*He moves to* JACKSON, *takes the lists from him, crosses again to* FREDDIE, *and hands the lists to him.*) And here are the lists of key words. And now, which hotel do you think ?
FREDDIE. Ooh, I don't know. What about the Splendide ?
BELMON. Splendid.
FREDDIE. They pronounce it Splendide, don't they ?
BELMON. Exactly—splen—excellent.

(*The front door bell rings.*)

JACKSON (*easing down* L.). It's just a suggestion ; but wouldn't it be a good idea if your friend Mr Ramshead pretended to be your servant ?

(GRUBB *enters up* R., *crosses the alcove and exits up* L. BABA *eases down* R.)

BELMON. A very good idea indeed, if Mr Ramshead wouldn't mind. It would obviate all difficulty with hotel servants at meal times. That is going to be your greatest difficulty—she can't eat. Now, if Mr Ramshead could wait on you . . .
FREDDIE (*turning to* BABA). Baba, do you think you could manage to pretend to be a servant ?
BABA. Well, I might try.
JACKSON. Well, it can't be very difficult. Just try to remember to call him "sir".
BABA. All right, sir. Yes, sir. Very good, sir, I will, sir.
FREDDIE. Oh, that's very good, isn't it ? You'd think he'd done it before. And now, hadn't we better meet the lady ?
BELMON. Well, no. Before you do, I want you to be thoroughly familiar with those words of command. Perhaps we might go over them together.

ACT I] THE PERFECT WOMAN 21

(GRUBB *enters up* L.)

GRUBB. Beg pardon, sir. Colonel Spindle is outside in his car.
FREDDIE. Not *the* Colonel Spindle?
BELMON. Yes. D'you know him?
FREDDIE. No.

(BABA *remonstrates with* FREDDIE.)

(*To* BABA.) Well, it helps the conversation.
BELMON (*turning to* GRUBB). Ask him to wait in the drawing room.
GRUBB. He won't come in, sir. He says that if you don't start at once, you will be late for the meeting, sir.
JACKSON (*looking at his watch*). By Jove, yes. It's five to seven already. (*He finishes his drink and places his glass on the table* R. *of the fireplace.*)
BELMON. Is it really? Well, will you go out to him, Jackson? Say I'm just coming.
JACKSON (*moving up* L.). Certainly. But be quick, my dear fellow. You know how impatient he is.

(*He exits up* L.)

BELMON. Oh, Grubb, these gentlemen will be remaining for a while; they won't require anything.
GRUBB. Very good, sir.

(*He exits up* L.)

BELMON. I can't stop now, but do have a good look at those lists, and when you can, go in and get the woman. (*He points up* C.) She is in my laboratory there.
FREDDIE. Hadn't you better introduce us?
BELMON. Quite unnecessary. You'll find her there—under a dust sheet. All you have to do is to uncover her, tell her to come with you, and she will obey.
FREDDIE. That sounds rather unconventional, doesn't it?
BELMON. Not at all; you'll soon get used to her. Oh, there's one thing—there are certain things that you must not ask her to do.
FREDDIE. Oh, I wouldn't. (*To* BABA.) Would I?
BABA. No.
BELMON. And there is one word especially that you must never use in her presence.
FREDDIE. I never use that one. Which one were you thinking of?
BELMON. That word is—love.
FREDDIE. Love?
BABA. Love?
BELMON. Yes. If she hears that word she defends herself in a most violent manner; so please be careful to avoid it.
FREDDIE. Oh, thanks for the warning. (*To* BABA.) No love.

(GRUBB *enters up* L.)

GRUBB. Beg pardon, sir. Dr Jackson is getting rather impatient.
BELMON. Yes, yes. I'm coming now.

(GRUBB *exits up* R.)

(*He trots to* FREDDIE *and shakes hands with him.*) I really can't stop now, gentlemen. (*He trots down* R. *to* BABA.) I do hope you will have an interesting week. (*He shakes hands with* BABA, *turns and trots up* C.)

(FREDDIE *and* BABA *fall in behind* BELMON *and trot round after him in single file until he exits.*)

There are not many men I would trust with my woman— (*he trots to the exit up* R., *realizes he is going the wrong way, wheels round and trots to the exit up* L.) but I think I can trust you. Well, good-bye.

(*He trots off up* L. FREDDIE *and* BABA *stop and wave to him from up* C.)

FREDDIE }
BABA   } (*together*). Good-bye, Professor—good-bye.

BABA. Very affable old party that, sir.
FREDDIE. Rather. Splendid judge of character. See the way he chose me for the job.
BABA. Yes, sir. (*He indicates the door up* C.) Well, that's where he said the woman is.
FREDDIE. Yes, that's where she is.
BABA. Hadn't you better go and get her?
FREDDIE. I think you'd better.
BABA (*moving down* L.). Why me?
FREDDIE. Well, you're my butler, aren't you?
BABA. No, sir, I'm your friend.
FREDDIE. Oh, I forgot that. (*He indicates the lists.*) Well, I think we'd better learn these first.
BABA. Well, that won't take you long, sir. You only want the key words.
FREDDIE (*moving down to* R. *of* BABA). Don't be silly. I couldn't learn this in a month of Sundays. Come on—halves, partner. (*He gives* BABA *half of the lists.*)
BABA (*taking the lists*). I don't want these, sir.
FREDDIE. Go on, you learn that half, I'll learn this.
BABA. This is like homework, this is.

(*Facing the audience and close together down* L., *they proceed to study the lists.*)

FREDDIE. Certainly is. Listen to this. " In the home. In the restaurant. At the station." The old boy's done it very thoroughly.
BABA. What have I got? " On the stairs. In the bedroom,

In the bathroom. In the..." My word! He's thought of everything, hasn't he?
FREDDIE. "Stand up. Sit down. Left. Right. Double-de-clutch."
BABA. Double-de-clutch? What's that?
FREDDIE. I don't know.
BABA. What does it mean?
FREDDIE. It's an order. It just says double-de-clutch, that's all.
BABA. Where does she do it?
FREDDIE. In an emergency.
BABA. Well, we mustn't take her into one of those.
FREDDIE. Oh, look. Movements for arms. " Up. Down. Clasp, slap, tickle." Surely the slap ought to come after the tickle. Shouldn't it?
BABA. Oh, sir, look what I've got.
FREDDIE. What?
BABA. Movements for legs.
FREDDIE. Any pictures?
BABA. No, sir, no. " Run. Up. Step. Walk. Down. Lift." What does she want to walk down the lift for.
FREDDIE. No, no. Walk, down, lift. Three different orders—that's all. Oh, look, we'll never learn all this. Keep it in your pocket and then we can refer to it when working. (*He puts his list in his pocket.*)

(BABA *puts his list in his pocket.*)

BABA (*pointing up* C.). She's in there.
FREDDIE. Yes, there she is. (*He takes hold of* BABA'S *right arm and leads him up* C.) In you go.
BABA. What?
FREDDIE. Yes, you go in. You've got the movements for legs. Take off the dust sheet and tell her to walk this way.
BABA. I'm not so sure about it, sir. Look here, we've got the money anyway, couldn't we...
FREDDIE. No, we couldn't. Go on, inside, and start her up.
BABA. Start her up?
FREDDIE. Yes, get her going.

(BABA *exits up* C.)

BABA (*off*). It's pitch dark in here.
FREDDIE. Well, put the lights on. Hurry up.
BABA (*off*). I can't find the switch.
FREDDIE. Well, look for it, you fool.

(*There is the sound of breaking glass, off up* C.)

(*He calls.*) Now what have you done?
BABA (*off; calling*). I think I've upset something in the conservatory.
FREDDIE. Baba, you're hopeless. I suppose I'd better...

BABA (*off ; calling*). Oh, sir.
FREDDIE. Now what ?
BABA (*off*). I've found something horrible.
  (BABA, *carrying a dummy hand, enters up* C.)
FREDDIE. What d'you mean you've found something horrible ?
BABA (*holding up the hand*). Look.
FREDDIE. Great Scot ! It's a hand—at least a sort of hand.
BABA. It *is* a hand—one of those the Professor's been cutting up.
FREDDIE. He wouldn't do such a thing—or would he ?
BABA. Exactly what those Professors do. They cut 'em up quite small.
FREDDIE. *What for ?*
BABA. For fun.
FREDDIE. But Professor Belmon doesn't cut 'em up, he builds 'em up.
BABA. Does he ?
FREDDIE. This must be one he's just started.
BABA. He hasn't got very far with it, has he ? (*He indicates his arm from the wrist to the shoulder.*) There's all this to come.
FREDDIE. Well, dash it all, he must start somewhere.
BABA. Fancy starting with her hand.
FREDDIE. Well, where would you start ?
BABA. Don't ask me, I've never made one.
FREDDIE. Look here, there must be lots more pieces lying around somewhere. I'll go and have a look. Jolly exciting.
  (*He exits up* C.)
(*Off.*) I shouldn't be surprised if . . . Ugh !
BABA (*backing to* L. *of the sofa ; calling*). What is it, sir ?
(FREDDIE *enters up* C. *He carries a dummy leg and " walks " it across the stage, chasing* BABA *down* C.)
FREDDIE (*moving to* BABA). Look, a woman's leg. I could tell with my eyes shut.
BABA. Put it down, sir. You don't know what we might find next. Drop it and let's go home.
FREDDIE. Don't be a fool. We haven't got a home.
BABA. Oh, I'd forgotten that.
FREDDIE (*trying reflexes on the leg*). Shows she's healthy.
BABA. Sir, you don't think that's the woman we've to take to the hotel ?
FREDDIE. Good heavens, I hope it's going to be in one piece. How can I go to an hotel with this, and say, " A double room, please."
BABA. It's going to be a bit of a job sticking these together.
FREDDIE (*giving* BABA *the leg*). Hold this, Baba. (*He moves to the door up* C. *and feels for the light switch.*) There must be a light somewhere.

BABA (*throwing the hand and leg on to the sofa*). I don't want these, sir.
FREDDIE (*finding the switch*). Yes, here it is—look. (*He switches on the laboratory light and looks off.*) Oh! (*He turns.*) It's there.
BABA. What, the woman he's cutting up?
FREDDIE. No, the one under the dust sheet.

(*He exits up* C.)

(*Off. Calling.*) It's in a wheel-chair contraption. I'll bring it out.
BABA (*moving* R. *and hiding on the stairs*). Oh, careful, sir, careful. I don't like it.

(FREDDIE *enters up* C., *pushing a wheel-chair in which* JOAN *is seated, covered by a dust sheet. She is in evening dress.*)

FREDDIE (*pushing the chair* C.). Bogey, bogey, bogey. Penny for the guy.
BABA. It might go off with a bang.
FREDDIE. There we are. Who's going to do the unveiling?
BABA. You are, sir. I'm only the butler.
FREDDIE (*moving* L. *of the wheel-chair*). Funny thing, when anything gets a bit sticky, you're always the butler, aren't you?
BABA. It's eerie.
FREDDIE. Go on, you're a funk. (*He raises the front of the dust sheet a few inches.*) It's only a dummy. Baba, look—a foot.
BABA (*moving* R. *of the wheel-chair*). Two foots.
FREDDIE (*raising the dust sheet a little higher*). Legs.
BABA. I wonder if it's all here?
FREDDIE. Bet it is. If those are there the rest ought to be. Let's have a look.

(BABA *and* FREDDIE *roll back the dust sheet which* FREDDIE *throws on to the easy chair down* L.)

Oh, Baba, look at that.
BABA. Oh, I'm glad I stayed.
FREDDIE (*surveying* JOAN). Doesn't he do 'em beautifully?
BABA. Tell you what, sir. I bet that old Professor gets lots of orders for these.
FREDDIE. You bet he does. There won't be a home without one. And to think I've got her for a whole week.
BABA (*picking up the dummy hand and leg from the sofa*). I wonder if I could fix these together. She'd like a bit of company, wouldn't she, sir?
FREDDIE. You mean you'd like a bit of company.
BABA. Well, look what you've got.
FREDDIE. Well, dash it all, it's only a figure.
BABA. I know, but what a figure. I only want the middle part really.
FREDDIE (*touching* JOAN's *cheek*). Baba.

BABA. Sir?
FREDDIE. Come and feel this.
BABA. What?
FREDDIE. Feel this.
BABA. What?
FREDDIE. Oh, the meat, the stuffing, what it's made of.

(BABA *throws the hand and leg on to the sofa, moves* R. *of the wheelchair and feels* JOAN'S *right cheek*.)

Isn't that lovely?
BABA. Well, it's like silk. What a wonderful material. (*He holds* JOAN'S *right ear*.) Oh, sir, if you shut your eyes and hold her ear, you might almost imagine she's real.
FREDDIE. Oh, yes, Baba. Oh, I'm going miles away.
BABA. Better come back now, sir. It's a pleasing little face, isn't it?
FREDDIE. It's a very nice face.
BABA. As faces go, of course.
FREDDIE. "As faces go." Don't be so condescending. What's wrong with it?
BABA. Well, it's not my type really. I prefer the nose a little more retrousse. (*He pushes* JOAN'S *nose up*.)
FREDDIE. No, no. That's snub. I'd rather have it more patrician, (*he presses* JOAN'S *nose down*) like that. She looks rather depressed, doesn't she?

(*They press the corners of* JOAN'S *mouth down*.)

Let's make her smile.

(*They push the corners of her mouth up*.)

BABA. Tell you what, sir, you hold it like that, and I'll make it permanent.
FREDDIE. How?
BABA. While it's warm, you know, press it into position.
FREDDIE. Here, don't muck it about, you'll smudge the whole thing.
BABA. Have you seen her eyes, sir?
FREDDIE. The one this side's a beauty.
BABA (*bending close to* JOAN). You know what I think? I think the Professor's done a slap-up job.

(JOAN *lifts her arm from the chair and slaps* BABA *with the back of her hand*.)

(*He staggers back, holding his face*.) Oh!
FREDDIE (*laughing*). Ha, ha, ha. That's made my day. It's your own fault, you told her to do it.
BABA (*holding his face*). I didn't say a thing.
FREDDIE. Yes, you did. You said a sla . . . (*He realizes he is*

about to make the same mistake as BABA.) Well, anyway, come on, we've got to get her out of this.

BABA. You lift her up and take her away. I'm not going to touch her. I hate the sight of her.

FREDDIE. What d'you mean, lift her up ? (*He lifts* JOAN'S *skirt a little.*) She's got a perfectly good pair of legs.

BABA. Now come away, sir. I'm surprised at you, sir.

FREDDIE. Ah, it's only a dummy. (*He lifts the skirt a little higher and feels* JOAN'S *calf.*) Oh, Baba, feel those. Look how he's made them. They even wobble at the back.

BABA (*moving in* R. *of* JOAN). Yes, they are a slap-up job.

(JOAN *lifts both her arms from the chair and slaps both the men's faces. They straighten up hurriedly.*)

FREDDIE (*stepping in front of* JOAN ; *to* BABA). Will you shut up saying that. Dammit, for two pins I'd give you a kick in the pants.

(JOAN *kicks* FREDDIE *in the pants and he staggers down* C.)

BABA (*taking the lists from his pocket and referring to them*). Here we are, sir, here we are. Page eight.

FREDDIE. Look here, we've got to be jolly careful what we say.

BABA. You're telling me.

FREDDIE. And there are certain things we mustn't say to her.

BABA (*rubbing his face*). Yes, I know one of them.

FREDDIE (*pointing to the lists*). And that's the other.

BABA. No, I don't want to say that.

FREDDIE. No, I've said it.

BABA. She's very heavy handed.

FREDDIE. You try her foot and see what that's like. (*He crosses* L. *below* JOAN *and avoids an imaginary kick.*) Now, wait a minute. We've got to get her out of that chair. (*He moves* L. *of the table* L.C. *To* JOAN.) Stand up.

(JOAN *rises.*)

(*To* BABA.) Jolly good, isn't it ? Not even a creak. He must keep it well oiled.

BABA (*crossing to* FREDDIE). Wasn't that smooth ? Almost human.

FREDDIE. Now—let me look at the notes. (*He takes out his list.*) Here we are. (*To* JOAN.) Right.

(JOAN *turns and faces* R.)

Now, wait a minute, let's see if we can make her walk.

(JOAN *starts to move* R., *bumping* BABA *as she passes.*)

Baba, look at that, it works. (*To* JOAN.) Left. (*He eases a little* L.C.)

(JOAN *faces the audience and moves towards the footlights.*)

(*To* JOAN.) Left.

(JOAN *turns and moves* C., *below* FREDDIE.)

(*To* JOAN.) Left.

(JOAN *turns and moves up* C., *collides with* FREDDIE *and stops with her back to the audience.* FREDDIE *staggers up* L.C.)

BABA. Now be careful, sir. You mustn't race her too much, her engine may not be run in.

FREDDIE. If we take her out on the street, she ought to have an " L " on her back. No, but seriously, who's going to do the running repairs, if anything goes wrong? There's no spanners or anything.

BABA. Nothing at all, sir.

FREDDIE (*to* JOAN). Turn round.

(JOAN *turns and faces the audience.*)

(*He moves to* L. *of* JOAN *and offers her his right arm.*) Now, take my arm.

(JOAN *does not move.*)

(*To* BABA.) She hasn't got that one. (*He refers to the lists. To* JOAN.) Arm up.

(JOAN *raises her right arm sideways so rapidly that* FREDDIE *is nearly bowled over.*)

Oh, so you want to play rough, eh? Well, we'll have to manhandle her. (*He grabs* JOAN'S *left arm.*)

BABA. Oh, do be careful, sir, don't break her.

FREDDIE. She'll give at the joints. (*He bends* JOAN'S *left arm into his right arm.*) That's better. How do I look, Baba?

BABA. I think you look wonderful, sir, wonderful. (*Longingly.*) I wish I had one.

FREDDIE. Well, come along, you can share this one.

BABA (*moving to* R. *of* JOAN *and facing down stage*). Can I really, sir?

FREDDIE. Yes, bend it at the joints.

(BABA *takes hold of* JOAN'S *right arm and bends it into his left arm.*)

Forward.

(FREDDIE *and* BABA *step off, but* JOAN *does not move and they nearly lay her face downwards on the floor. They stand her upright and release her arms.*)

BABA. What we ought to have said was—walk.

(JOAN *starts to move down* C.)

FREDDIE. That's about the only thing that's left.

(JOAN *turns* L.)

ACT I] THE PERFECT WOMAN

Hey! Look out, she's off again.
(*To* JOAN.) Left.
    (JOAN *turns and moves up* L.)
Left.
    (JOAN *turns and moves* C.)
Right.
(JOAN *turns.* FREDDIE *and* BABA *catch her and each takes an arm. They all three move up* C. *in line.*)
Right.
    (*They all three turn and exit up* L.)

      CURTAIN.

ACT II

SCENE.—*Bedroom No. 29 at the Hotel Splendide. 8-30 p.m. the same evening.*

The room is large and luxurious. The door, which opens inwards, and bears the number "29" on the outside, is in the R. *side of a small alcove up* L. *There is a door leading to the bathroom* L. *and a large window up* R. *A double bed, with a bedside cabinet and upright chair below it, stands* R. *The dressing-table is in front of the window, the wardrobe is against the wall up* C. *and there is a chest of drawers above the door* L. *A circular table, with an armchair* R. *of it stands* L.C. *The alcove is furnished with a small table and upright chair ; a similar chair stands below the door* L., *and there is a luggage rack at the foot of the bed. The floor is carpeted and the windows are curtained. The room is lit by a centre pendant, a table-lamp on the bedside cabinet, a pair of small candle-lamps on the dressing-table and wall brackets on the wall,* R. *and* L. *of the head of the bed, and* R. *and* L. *of the door* L.

(See the Ground Plan at the end of the Play.)

When the CURTAIN *rises, the stage is in darkness. Almost immediately,* FARINI, *an expansive Italian, the Maitre d'hotel, enters up* L., *and the light from the corridor illuminates the door, clearly showing the number "29".*

FARINI *(looking at the number on the door).* Ah, ecco numero ventinove. *(From the switches by the door, he puts on the wall brackets, the pendant, and dressing-table lights. He then eases* C. *and looks around, rubbing his hands and admiring the effect and the room.)*

(WINKEL, *a serious, German-Swiss waiter, enters up* L.)

Capite, il signore che arrivera stasera . . .
WINKEL. Ni' I ka' nid Italinische spreche.
FARINI. Come. No parlo Italiano ?
WINKEL. Nein. Aber I can very goot Englische spreche.
FARINI. Si ? And why you can not Italian ?
WINKEL. Because I have not it yet gelearnt.
FARINI. In which case it is no goot. You should spika all language lika me. I spika everybody perfect. If he come from England I spika. If he come from Holland I spika.
WINKEL. Russia ?
FARINI. I no spika. *(He moves to the window up* R. *and partly draws the curtains.)*

30

[To face page 30 "The Perfect Woman"]

ACT II]   THE PERFECT WOMAN   31

WINKEL. Me not. Aber some day I speak too. Very goot Englische I understand.
FARINI (*moving* R. *of* WINKEL). You never bin waiter before?
WINKEL. Nein.
FARINI (*adjusting* WINKEL'S *coat*). What then?
WINKEL. I was business man, but I had a bankrupture.
FARINI (*moving down* C.). Ah. Understand this. (*He beckons* WINKEL *to come to him*.) Here coma tonight Mr Cavendish—very good guest, spend a lotta money. He coma tonight wis his wifa, his brida, you know?
WINKEL (*moving* L. *of* FARINI). No, I do not know it.
FARINI. You do not know. You understand English, and you not know what is the brida.
WINKEL. Ven she come I vill her know.
FARINI (*crossing* WINKEL *to the chest of drawers*). When she come —si, si, when she come. But you know what it is the brida? (*He arranges the flowers in the vase on the chest of drawers.*)
WINKEL. Ja. Ja. Shoon goot. What make they here?
FARINI (*turning*). Maka? I do not know what they maka. They don't maka nothing. They come here for sleep; for pensione.
WINKEL. Tonight they come.
FARINI. I tell you. (*He moves* L. *of* WINKEL.) Tonight they coma and wish a nica suite.
WINKEL. Ja. Ja. Apple strudel, rice pudding.
FARINI. No, they want a suite. Bedroom, saloon, bath, hum hum, everything. And you know, we have not a suite. Alla suite taken. We cannot giva the suite.
WINKEL. They cannot have it.
FARINI. They must have it.
WINKEL. Ja, I understand. They cannot, aber they must—huh?
FARINI. They must have this room. And if they want meals here, you serve it you know.
WINKEL. Goot.
FARINI. If they want you bring foot.
WINKEL (*looking at his foot*). Foot?
FARINI. No. (*He stamps on* WINKEL'S *foot.*) Foot. (*He points to his mouth.*) Eat. Ham ham. (*He points to his stomach.*) Manjare. Ay, ay ay ay ay ay. (*He moves to the door* L., *opens it a little and switches on the bathroom light.*) And you are very careful. (*He turns and moves* L. *of* WINKEL.) Mr Cavendish very important guest. He coma very often. Now go. (*He turns* WINKEL *and pushes him towards the door up* L.) Bring flowers, bring everything. *Trubito.*

(WINKEL *exits up* L. FARINI *sings* "La Donna Mobile" *softly to himself, as he moves to the bed, straightens the bed cover and then switches on the lamp on the bedside cabinet.* FREDDIE *enters up* L., *turns and speaks off through the door to* JOAN.)

FREDDIE. Walk.

(JOAN *enters up* L.)

Stop.

(JOAN *stops*.)

Right.

(JOAN *faces the audience.* FREDDIE *moves down* C., *and for the moment does not see* FARINI.)

FARINI. Ah, Mr Cavendish.
FREDDIE (*startled*). Ah, Farini.
FARINI. Congratulatione.
FREDDIE. Congratulaché what?
FARINI. Er—congratulations.
FREDDIE. Congratulations—what for?
FARINI. On your marriage.
FREDDIE (*easing to the door* L.). Oh, yes, I'd forgotten all about it. Thanks very much, Farini.

(*He exits* L.)

FARINI (*easing* R.C.; *to* JOAN). And, Madame, I am charmed. This is your room. Will you please walk in.

(JOAN *moves down* L. *and is nearly at the footlights when* FREDDIE *enters hurriedly* L.)

FREDDIE (*to* JOAN). Stop.

(JOAN *stops, and* FARINI *looks bewildered.*)

FARINI. Sir, you not lika this room?
FREDDIE (*moving above* JOAN *to* C.). Oh, yes, I do. Yes, this is my favourite room, Farini.
FARINI. Oh, I am so pleased.
FREDDIE. Yes, it's grand. There's so much room to turn round.

(JOAN *about turns*.)

FARINI. To turn round?

(JOAN *turns and faces up stage*.)

FREDDIE. Yes. (*He watches* JOAN *out of the corner of his eye*.) Yes, I said—turn round.

(JOAN *turns and faces the audience.* FREDDIE *takes the list of instructions from his pocket and refers to it*.)

FARINI. Of course, I heard you, sir, you know. I am sorry, but it was impossible to give you a suite. Alla suite taken. But here, sir, you have a large room, (*he half turns away from* FREDDIE, *indicating the room with a sweep of his arm*) where you can turn round and round and round.

(JOAN *turns each time* FARINI *says* "*round*". FREDDIE *move quickly to* FARINI.)

FREDDIE (*desperately*). Stop.

(JOAN *stops, facing the audience*. FARINI *regards* FREDDIE *with astonishment*.)

I understand exactly what you mean, but my wife doesn't like it. It makes her giddy.

FARINI (*moving to the chair below the bed*). Oh, pardon, Madame. (*He indicates the chair*.) Would Madame not care to . . . ?

FREDDIE (*quickly*). Don't say it. Never ask my wife to—er . . . when she's standing up. (*He moves to the armchair* L.C.) Madame's very particular about her seat. (*He moves the armchair to* L. *of* JOAN.) Are you all *right*, dear?

(JOAN *turns and faces* R.)

Would you like to sit down?

(JOAN *sits in the armchair*.)

(*He bends over her*.) What, dear? I'll tell him. (*To* FARINI.) She likes this room very much indeed, Farini. Now don't you worry about us. We shall be all . . . You know what I mean.

FARINI. Oh, certainly, sir. (*He eases* R.C.) I quite understand. And if you would prefer to have your meals in the private . . .

FREDDIE (*moving* C.). Where? No, thanks, we'd rather have them in here, thank you.

FARINI. The waiter has orders to attend you only.

FREDDIE. No waiters.

FARINI. But who . . . ?

FREDDIE. My friend can look after us.

FARINI. Your friend?

FREDDIE. Yes, my best man. He's just seeing about the luggage.

FARINI. Your best man on your wedding night?

FREDDIE. Oh, yes, it's often done. I'm very sorry, but I can't stand waiters.

(JOAN *rises*.)

I can't sit down and watch

(JOAN *sits*.)

a waiter bobbing up and down.

(JOAN *bobs up and down*.)

I simply can't sit down and watch it.

(JOAN *sits still*.)

34   THE PERFECT WOMAN   [ACT II

FARINI (*moving in* R. *of* FREDDIE). You can't sit down while the waiter is . . .

FREDDIE (*putting his hand over* FARINI'S *mouth*). No, no, I know just what you were going to say.

FARINI. Very well, sir. I myself will serve you and stop the waiter bo . . .

FREDDIE (*interrupting*). Tell me outside, there's a good fellow. (*He takes* FARINI *by the arm and leads him up* C.)

(BABA, *carrying a small suitcase, enters up* L., *crosses below* FREDDIE *and* FARINI, *and places the suitcase on the luggage rack at the foot of the bed.*)

Ah, this is my *best man*.

(BABA *and* FARINI *bow to each other.*)

My best man.

BABA. I've brought the luggage, *Freddie*.
FREDDIE. Thanks old chap.
BABA. That's all right, old man.
FREDDIE. Where did you get it?
BABA. In the next room.
FARINI. *Pardonez*—shall I tell the porter to bring up the other baggage?
FREDDIE. The what?
FARINI. The other baggage—the beeg baggage?
FREDDIE. Oh! The beeg . . . (*To* BABA.) Where's the beeg baggage?
BABA. It's coming on in advance later, sir.
FREDDIE (*to* FARINI). It's coming on in advance later.
FARINI. Very good, sir. Very good. But has Madame all that she wants for tonight?
FREDDIE. Madame has everything. A tooth brush, a what's it and me.
FARINI (*bowing deeply*). *Signori, Signora. Bueno notches, bueno notches.*

FREDDIE }
BABA   } (*together ; bowing*). *Bueno* . . .

(FARINI *exits up* L. FREDDIE *moves below the bed.*)

FREDDIE (*sitting on the downstage edge of the bed*). Phew! You know, this is getting me down. Lock the door and keep those monkeys out of here.

BABA (*moving to the door up* L. *and locking it*). Why, I thought you were getting on splendidly, sir.

FREDDIE. It all looks so damned suspicious. That thing sitting there, saying nothing.

BABA (*moving* C.). Yes, it is a bit unnatural. You don't think he suspected anything?

FREDDIE. I don't know, but it's got me like this. (*He raises his hands, which are trembling.*) I don't know where I am.
BABA. Well, you're over the worst for tonight.
FREDDIE. What d'you mean " over the worst " ? What about this dinner we've got to have ?
BABA. Don't worry about that, sir. I'll eat her share.
FREDDIE. No, no. Let's cut dinner.
BABA. We'll have to cut it, if we're going to share it.
FREDDIE (*laughing mirthlessly*). Shut up. I mean, let's cut dinner out altogether.
BABA. Oh, no. You must keep up your strength, sir. So must I.
FREDDIE. Well, order some chicken or something.
BABA. Some chicken *and* something.
FREDDIE. Yes. A bottle of wine, eh ? But keep the waiter out. I don't want him to see her.
BABA. Leave the waiter to me, sir. I can handle waiters.
FREDDIE. Jove ! I must have a wash. I'm all hot and sticky with nerves.
BABA (*pointing to the door* L.). There's the bathroom, sir.
FREDDIE. I don't know how we're going to get through this thing tonight, I don't really.
BABA. Don't worry, sir. Don't worry.
FREDDIE (*rising*). I'm worried to death.
BABA. You forget that I am with you, sir.
FREDDIE (*crossing to the door* L.). Yes, that's half my worry.

(*He exits* L.)

(*Off. Calling.*) Baba. Have we got a nail brush ?
BABA (*moving to the suitcase*). I don't quite know what we've got, sir. (*He opens the suitcase, and reveals that it is empty except for a nail brush.*) Oh, well, by an extraordinary coincidence, sir, that's just what we have got.

(*He crosses to the door* L. *and exits.* JOAN *rises quickly, runs to the door up* L., *unlocks it, takes the key from the lock and hides it under the bed. She then moves to the armchair* L.C. *and sits as before.* WINKEL, *carrying a bunch of flowers, enters up* L., *moves* R. *of* JOAN *and stares at her, puzzled, for several seconds.*)

WINKEL. You like something ?

(JOAN *just stares for a few moments, then realizing that* FREDDIE *and* BABA *are not present, shakes her head.*)

If dere is anything I can do for Madame, or . . .
JOAN (*in a loud stage whisper*). No, thank you.
WINKEL. You lost the voice ?

(JOAN *looks towards the door* L.)

I bring blumen. (*He holds out the bunch of flowers.*) Will Madame arrange these or . . . ?

JOAN. Yes. Put them down. Go away.
WINKEL. Go ? Go ? Where ?
JOAN (*glancing fearfully over her shoulder, in terror of being heard*). Don't talk.
WINKEL. Pardon. Not to talk ?
JOAN. No. My husband doesn't like people to talk to me. He's very jealous.
WINKEL. Yallous ? What is " yallous " ?
JOAN. Don't talk. He'll kill you if you talk to me.
WINKEL (*alarmed*). Gill me ? Aber, he can not. I am Swiss. Neutral. (*He raises his hand.*) If Madame would like, I . . .
JOAN. Shush.

(JOAN *suddenly stiffens.* WINKEL *shrugs his shoulders and eases towards the door up* L. BABA *enters* L.)

BABA (*to* WINKEL). Hello.

(WINKEL *stops and turns.*)

WINKEL. Hello.
BABA. What do you want ?
WINKEL. Noding.
BABA. Well, you've got it. Go on, out you go and take it with you.
WINKEL (*holding the flowers behind his back*). I only come to ask, sir, what you for dinner like.
BABA. What have you got there ?
WINKEL. Flowers. I think you like them for dinner.
BABA. What d'you think I am, a Colorado beetle ?

(WINKEL *moves down* C. BABA *eases above* JOAN.)

WINKEL. I think, perhaps, Madame, she like . . .
BABA. Come on, what's up ?
WINKEL. Noding's up.
BABA. Out with it, what were you doing while I was in there ?
WINKEL. Noding, truly noding. I do not speak with Madame.
BABA. Why not ? (*He crosses above* WINKEL *to down* R.)
WINKEL. She says that . . .

(JOAN *shakes her head and makes signs to* WINKEL *not to say any more.* BABA *does not see this.*)

I mean I tink you it would not like.
BABA (*turning*). You're quite right. I it would not like, and a kick in the pants you'll get if I catch you talking to her, you understand ?
WINKEL. No, sir.
BABA (*moving* R. *of* WINKEL). Yes, sir. (*He takes the flowers from* WINKEL *and places them on the luggage rack.*) Any talking to be

Act II]   THE PERFECT WOMAN   37

done, I'll do it. Now about dinner. We don't want much. We're not hungry.
WINKEL. Not hungry?
BABA. No. We'll just have a light repast. Just a little soup, fish, chicken, joint, sweet, dessert, coffee and anything else that occurs to you.
WINKEL. Yes, sir. (*He moves up* L.) Is that all, sir?
BABA. Yes, I tell you we're not hungry. Oh, and perhaps a bottle of wine and a couple of dozen bottles of beer.
WINKEL. Yes, sir. You're not thirsty too, eh?
BABA (*moving to* WINKEL). That's enough from you, George. Is your name George?
WINKEL. No, sir.
BABA. What is your name?
WINKEL. Winkel, sir.
BABA. Winkel?
WINKEL. Yes, sir.
BABA. Well, back to your shell, Winkel. Allez, scram.

(*He takes* WINKEL *by the arm and leads him to the door up* L. WINKEL *exits.* FREDDIE *enters* L., *carrying a towel.*)

(*He moves* L. *of the bed.*) It's all right, sir. I've ordered the dinner.
FREDDIE (*wiping his hands*). Ordered it, why? Has the waiter been in here?
BABA. Yes, but he's not coming again.
FREDDIE. But did he see her?
BABA. I think he's got a kind of roving eye for Miss Rowbotham, or whatever her name is.
FREDDIE. No!
BABA (*picking up the flowers*). Well, look what he brought her.
FREDDIE. Good gracious! You don't think he made any sort of proposition to her?
BABA. I wouldn't put it past him, you know these Americans.
FREDDIE. One thing—(*he throws the towel off through the door* L.) she couldn't give him any encouragement.
BABA. I'm not so sure.
FREDDIE (*crossing to the bed*). Don't be silly. (*He sits on the downstage edge of the bed.*) She can't talk.
BABA. Well, that is encouragement. She can't say "no".
FREDDIE. Oh, she's becoming a frightful responsibility, Baba.
BABA (*moving to the table in the alcove*). She is. I'm beginning to realise what mothers have to go through. (*He puts the flowers in the vase on the table*).
FREDDIE. There's another thing that's worrying me. This luggage business—three of us here, with only one small suitcase. It looks so bad.
BABA (*easing* C.). Leave it to me, sir, I can soon pop along the passage and get some more.

FREDDIE. No.
BABA. I could get you a set of golf clubs, sir.
FREDDIE. No.
BABA. I know, sir—let me ring up cook and get some of your stuff from home.
FREDDIE. D'you think she'd work it for us?
BABA (*moving to the chair below the bed*). Yes, sir, yes. She'll do anything for me—I'll get her. (*He sits.*)
FREDDIE. Oh, it's like that, is it?
BABA (*lifting the telephone receiver*). What shall I ask her to send, sir? (*He dials a number.*)
FREDDIE. Oh, a couple of trunks.
BABA. Anything in them?
FREDDIE. Two of everything. (*He takes the lists from his pocket.*) I'm going to learn some of these orders and get this thing moving. I'll have it standing on its head before I've finished with it.
BABA (*into the telephone*). Hello, is that Lady Boagle's house? . . . This is me speaking. I want to speak to Mrs Glendower-Evans— the cook . . . Oh, is that you, Maggie? . . . Yes, you're quite right, this is your Albert, your oochie-poochie, Maggie waggie . . . Yes. I've missed you, too. It hasn't been the same without you, Maggie waggie . . .
FREDDIE. Oh, would you and Maggie waggie like to be alone?
BABA (*into the telephone*). Well, what about next Saturday? . . . Same time, same place . . . Right-ho, then . . . Good-bye, good-bye, good-bye.

(*He blows kisses into the receiver, and is about to replace it when* FREDDIE *interrupts him.*)

FREDDIE. Hey, hold on.
BABA. Hold on?
FREDDIE. Trunks.
BABA (*into the telephone*). Oh, I want trunks.
FREDDIE (*exasperated*). Oh, no.
BABA (*into the telephone*). Oh, hello. Maggie—are you there? . . . Good. I want you to send round a pair of trunks for Mr Freddie . . . No, not drunks—trunks. What he puts his things in . . . No, not bathing trunks—leather trunks, luggage trunks . . .
FREDDIE. Oh, can't she understand English?
BABA (*into the telephone*). Yes, send them to the Hotel Splendide. That's French for splendid . . . Don't let old Goofy know . . . No, give her a kick in the pants. (*He laughs.*) Ha, ha, ha . . .
FREDDIE. Yes, give her two from me.

(BABA *stops laughing abruptly, looks alarmed, and signals to* FREDDIE *to be quiet.*)

BABA (*into the telephone*). No, my lady. No, my lady . . . No,

it's not me speaking . . . I don't know where Mr Freddie is, my lady. (*He replaces the receiver.*)
FREDDIE. Was that auntie?
BABA (*rising*). The last part was. She must have cut in.
FREDDIE. No, but did she hear where we were?
BABA. No, it's all right, I fooled her, sir. She asked me if it was me speaking, and I said "no", then she asked if you were with me and I said "yes". I threw dust in the old bird's eyes.
FREDDIE. She may get it out of cook.
BABA. Oh, no, sir. Maggie wouldn't give anything away—she's Welsh. (*He crosses to* L.) Don't you worry about it, sir. I feel sure that nothing more can possibly happen tonight.

(*There is a knock at the door up* L. *and* FARINI *enters, carrying a tray with a silver bowl of soup, ladle, and three soup plates on it. He places the tray and its contents on the table in the alcove. He is followed by* WINKEL, *who carries a small table set for dinner for three.*)

FARINI. Dinner is served.
FREDDIE (*rising*). Nothing more—can happen tonight.

(WINKEL *places the table down* C.)

FARINI. I hope you are all ready.
FREDDIE. We're ready for anything, Farini.
FARINI (*moving above the table* C.). Will Madame sit in the middle?
FREDDIE (*easing down* R.). Will Madame sit in the middle? Yes, I think Madame could *stand* a little food.

(JOAN *rises.*)

BABA. I'm sure she could—that's right.

(JOAN *turns and faces up stage.*)

FREDDIE. She's quite hungry after her *walk*.

(JOAN *moves up* C.)

FARINI (*easing below the bed*). Madame likes walking?
BABA. With the petrol cut, what's left.

(JOAN, *nearly at the wardrobe, turns and faces* R.)

FREDDIE. Yes. What is *left*.

(JOAN *turns, faces front, and moves down* C.)

You can't stop——

(JOAN *stops.* WINKEL *brings the chair from the alcove and places it above* JOAN *just in time for her to sit on it.*)

—her taking exercise.

WINKEL. Will Madame sit ?

(FREDDIE *and* BABA *rush to* JOAN, *who sits in the chair* WINKEL *has placed for her.* FREDDIE *and* BABA *each grab* WINKEL *by a hand and congratulate him.* FARINI *moves to the chair below the bed and places it* R. *of the table* C. *for* FREDDIE.)

FARINI. Sir, your chair. Winkel, serve the soup. I hope you will like it, Madame.

(WINKEL *moves to the table in the alcove and serves out three plates of soup.* BABA *places the armchair from* L.C., L. *of the table* C., *and sits.*)

FREDDIE. I'm sure she will.

(FARINI *moves to the table in the alcove, picks up one plate of soup, moves to the table* C. *and places the soup in front of* JOAN. WINKEL *places the two other plates of soup in front of* FREDDIE *and* BABA.)

WINKEL (*as he puts the plates on the table* C. ; *very abruptly*). Soup. Soup.

(FARINI *grabs* WINKEL *to remonstrate with him and they move up* C., *arguing.* FREDDIE *and* BABA *grab their spoons and start to eat* JOAN'S *soup whilst* FARINI *is otherwise occupied. They just finish it in time.* FARINI *moves to the table and does a double-take as he notices that* JOAN'S *plate is empty.*)

FARINI. Madame eat her soup already ?
BABA }
FREDDIE } (*together*). So she has.
FREDDIE (*gulping*). Without a spoon, too.
BABA. Madame's very fond of soup, Farini. She once won a soup-eating championship.
FREDDIE. That's it, she was Miss Cockaleekie of nineteen-forty-seven—Miss Turtle the year before.
WINKEL (*moving to the table* C.). Madame more cock-a-leekie like ? (*He takes* JOAN'S *plate.*)
FREDDIE (*rising angrily*). No.

(BABA *rises, and he and* FREDDIE *grab* FARINI *and* WINKEL, *and lead them up* C., *shouting.*)

Didn't I tell you no waiters ?
BABA (*shouting*). I told you not to talk to her.

(JOAN *takes advantage of their lack of attention to eat* BABA'S *soup.*)

(*He moves to his chair* L. *of the table* C. *and notices his soup has disappeared.*) My cock-a-leekie's leaked.
FREDDIE (*moving* L. *of the table* C.). Let's get rid of it. (*He hands his plate to* FARINI.)

(BABA *hands his plate to* WINKEL. JOAN *takes* FREDDIE'S *bread and bites a piece out of it.* WINKEL *exits up* L. *with the plates.*)

We'll forget the soup. (*He turns back to the table and notices his bread is missing. He turns to* FARINI.) Farini, where's my bread?

(JOAN *replaces the bread.*)

FARINI (*looking at the table* C.). It's there, sir.
FREDDIE. Well, someone's been at it.

(WINKEL *enters up* L., *carrying three plates of chicken.*)

WINKEL (*moving to the table* C.). Huhne, huhne, huhne. (*He places the plates in front of* JOAN, FREDDIE *and* BABA.)

(FREDDIE *and* BABA *resume their seats at the table.*)

BABA. Huhne?
FARINI. Huhne?
FREDDIE. What's huhne?
WINKEL. Ja. (*He makes flapping motions with his arms.*) Chuck-chuck. Chuck-chuck.
FARINI (*correcting* WINKEL). Sapristi—Chicken. (*Disgustedly.*) Huhne.

(*He takes* WINKEL *up* L. *to put him wise in no uncertain manner, and places the soup plate on the table in the alcove.* WINKEL *exits up* L. FREDDIE *and* BABA *quickly eat* JOAN'S *chicken.* FARINI *moves to the table and sees that* JOAN'S *plate is empty.*)

Madame finished her chicken already?
FREDDIE (*frantically*). Yes, she was champion chicken eater, too.
BABA. Yes. Miss Buff Orpington of nineteen forty-eight.
FARINI (*peering at* JOAN'S *face*). Is Madame not well?
FREDDIE. She always looks like that with a headache.

(FARINI *passes his hand in front of* JOAN'S *face and is puzzled by her lack of reaction.*)

FARINI. But she does not move?
FREDDIE. She never moves with a headache.
BABA. There's a very simple explanation for that, Farini.
FREDDIE (*puzzled*). Is there?
BABA. My friend here has mesmerized her. It's a cure.

(WINKEL, *carrying two dishes of vegetables, enters up* L.)

FARINI (*easing* L. *of* JOAN). Really?

(WINKEL *moves up* R. *of* JOAN.)

FREDDIE. Oh, I often do it. I put the fluence on like this. (*He makes a few passes with his hands.*)

(WINKEL *comes under the influence and starts to sway to and fro with closed eyes.*)

And then I say, " Away headache, away headache, away headache, away headache."

FARINI (*noticing* WINKEL). Winkel, what do you do?

BABA (*astonished*). You *can* do it, sir.

(FREDDIE *and* BABA *rise, and with* FARINI *crowd round* WINKEL *and try to wake him by slapping his face and shaking him. During the confusion,* JOAN *eats* FREDDIE'S *chicken. They succeed in waking* WINKEL, *who moves to the alcove and puts the dishes on the table.*)

FREDDIE (*resuming his seat* R. *of the table* C.). I can do it, it must be a gift. (*He makes a gesture over the table.*) All I did was . . . (*He notices his chicken has disappeared.*) Farini—was that chicken quite fresh?

(BABA *resumes his seat* L. *of the table* C.)

FARINI. Certainly, sir.

FREDDIE. Well, it's flown off somewhere. (*He looks under the table and around his chair.*)

FARINI. Can I get you some more chicken?

FREDDIE (*wearily*). No, thank you.

FARINI. How about *glace a la maison*?

FREDDIE. Oh, glace a la anything—I don't care.

FARINI. That is—ice cream with shredded cocoanut—then strawberries on top of that and whipped cream all round it.

(JOAN *surreptitiously licks her lips in anticipation.*)

FREDDIE. No thanks, Farini. We've had it.

FARINI. No, sir. You have not had it yet.

FREDDIE (*to* BABA). Oh—would you explain to the gentleman what I'm talking about.

BABA. Farini—my friend means we don't want any more to eat, thank you.

FARINI (*easing* R. *of* JOAN). But—no coffee, no . . .

(WINKEL *moves above* JOAN.)

FREDDIE. Nothing. We couldn't stand another thing.

(*At the word* "*stand*", JOAN *rises.* FREDDIE *and* BABA *hastily rise, and* WINKEL *takes* JOAN'S *chair and returns it to its former place in the alcove.* FARINI *fusses about getting the table* C. *ready for removal.* WINKEL *moves to the table* C., *picks it up, turns and exits with it up* L.)

FARINI. Please ring if you want anything.

FREDDIE. No, no. We've got everything, and we're going to bed, thank you. (*He returns his chair to its place down* R.)

ACT II] THE PERFECT WOMAN 43

FARINI (*looking doubtfully at* BABA). Your friend?
FREDDIE. My friend?
FARINI. The best man. Where does he sleep?
FREDDIE. He sleeps . . . (*He catches* BABA'S *eye.*)

(BABA *motions towards the door* L.)

Oh, in the bathroom.
FARINI (*very puzzled*). In the bathroom?
BABA. Yes. It's an old English custom.
FREDDIE. It's often done.
FARINI. On your vedding night?

(WINKEL *enters up* L.)

FREDDIE. Yes, I never do anything without his advice.
WINKEL. I like to be best man, too.
FARINI (*moving quickly up* L.). Winkel.

(WINKEL *picks up the tray, plates, etc., from the table in the alcove.*)

FREDDIE (*moving angrily up* L.). Get out of here.
BABA. Disgraceful.

(FARINI *hustles* WINKEL *and they both exit up* L. *There is a pause as* FREDDIE *turns and moves down* R.C.)

FREDDIE. At last.

(WINKEL, *carrying a basket filled with bottles, enters up* L.)

WINKEL. Drinks.
FREDDIE (*shouting*). Get out.

(WINKEL *places the basket on the table in the alcove and exits hurriedly up* L.)

Oh, Baba, I don't think I can stand any more of this.

(JOAN *sneezes.*)

BABA }
FREDDIE } (*together*). Bless you.

FREDDIE. I'm going to bed. If anybody wants me, I'm asleep and I'm not to be disturbed, see?
BABA. What about the wine?
FREDDIE (*taking off his jacket*). I'll have it in bed. (*He throws his jacket over the foot of the bed.*)
BABA. What about her nibs?
FREDDIE. Oh, let her stay there.
BABA. But you can't do that, sir. You'll have to put her to bed.
FREDDIE. Where?
BABA (*indicating the bed*). There.
FREDDIE. And where am I going to sleep?
BABA. Same place.

FREDDIE. I am not sleeping with a lot of nuts and bolts.
BABA. But it's the proper thing to do, sir. Dash it all, even a dummy has its rights. After all, sir, you are the bridegroom. What's the chambermaid going to say when she comes in, in the morning and sees you in bed and your bride standing in the middle of the room?
FREDDIE. She'll probably think we're being modern.
BABA. You leave this to me, sir. (*To* JOAN.) Walk. Stop.

(JOAN *moves down* C. *one pace and stops*.)

FREDDIE. Here. I don't want you giving orders. If I'm the bridegroom, I'll order my own wife about.
BABA. Very well, sir. You carry on.
FREDDIE. Something you haven't thought of. What's this dress going to look like in the morning, when she's been sleeping in it all night?
BABA. She's not going to sleep in it all night. You've got to give her orders to take it off.
FREDDIE. Don't be indecent, Baba. (*He pauses*.) Oh, all right, then. You look the other way, even a dummy may have feelings. (*To* JOAN. Undress. (*He turns away*.)

(JOAN *does not move*.)

BABA. No visible effect, sir.
FREDDIE (*moving above* JOAN). No, she's used to the Professor doing it. (*He examines the back of* JOAN'S *dress*.) Poppers. Good. (*He unfastens* JOAN'S *dress*.) Your portion.

(BABA *moves* L. *of* JOAN.)

(*He moves* R. *of* JOAN.) On the word three, Baba.

(BABA *takes hold of the left shoulder of the dress, and* FREDDIE *the right shoulder of it*.)

One—two—three—down.

(*They slip* JOAN'S *dress down, revealing her glamorous undies*.)

Oh, Baba, doesn't he finish them off beautifully? I thought it was going to be one of those canvas bodies, with the sawdust coming out. (*He surveys* JOAN *back and front*.) He's finished it all round the back as well. New Look, and everything.
BABA. Lift her up, sir, and I'll take this away.
FREDDIE (*moving behind* JOAN *and lifting her*). It's like a jelly baby.
BABA (*picking up* JOAN'S *dress*). I'd no idea it was such a business. I wonder they ever bother to get dressed at all. (*He puts the dress on the armchair* L.C.)
FREDDIE. Come on, let's get the rest off. A little strap hanging.

On the word three, Baba. One—to—er—wait a minute, Baba. What are we going to put on her? She hasn't got a nightie.
BABA. I've got half a pair of pyjamas.
FREDDIE. What's the good of half a pair? Why didn't you bring a full pair, then you could have lent her half?
BABA. Which half, sir?
FREDDIE. We won't go into that now. Well, she can't go to bed in nothing.
BABA. Good Lord, no, sir. You might get mixed up in the works.
FREDDIE. Well, she'll have to go as she is, that's all. It will look like a nightie up to there.
BABA. All right, sir, give her the orders.
FREDDIE (to JOAN). Now, get into bed.

(JOAN *does not move*.)

BABA. That's no good, sir. Got the list?
FREDDIE. Yes. Never answers to a reasonable one, does she? (*He takes the list from his pocket and refers to it.*) In the bedroom—no, that's no good. Here we are. Lie down.

(JOAN *lies flat on the floor*. BABA *and* FREDDIE *help catch her just in time to put her down carefully*.)

No, not there, dear—on the bed.

(JOAN *does not move*.)

Now, what's the chambermaid going to say in the morning if she sees her lying down there?
BABA. We can't have her lying there. We'll have to move her ourselves.

(FREDDIE *turns back the bedclothes, then assisted by* BABA, *lifts* JOAN *and puts her on the bed, but with her feet at the head of it*.)

FREDDIE. Baba, wrong way round.
BABA. That's easy, sir, just turn the bed round.
FREDDIE. Don't be silly. If we turn the bed round, she'll still be the wrong way round.
BABA. No, sir, she can't move.
FREDDIE. Oh, don't try and work it out. Come round here.

(*They lift* JOAN *and reverse her so that her head is now on the pillow*. FREDDIE *covers her with the bedclothes. They both move above the bed*, FREDDIE R. *of* BABA, *and survey* JOAN.)

BABA. Looks better upside down, doesn't she, sir?
FREDDIE. I do hope that she doesn't wear out before the end of the week.
BABA. I think the Professor's been very thorough. (*He lifts the bedclothes and looks closely at* JOAN.) Every detail as far as I can see.

FREDDIE (*sharply*). *Baba.* My bath, please.
BABA (*crossing to the door* L.). Oh, of course. I'd forgotten it was Friday.

(*He exits* L.)

FREDDIE (*to* JOAN). I shan't be a moment. (*He moves to the door up* L. *to see if it is locked, and notices the key is missing. He moves down* C. *and calls.*) Baba.
BABA (*off; calling*). Yes, sir.
FREDDIE. Where's the key?
BABA. In the door, sir. I left it there.
FREDDIE. Well, it's not there now. Come and have a look.
BABA. That's funny. I left it there.

(*He enters* L.)

Your bath's running.
FREDDIE. I'm not sure that we oughtn't to give the lady a bath. What do you think?

(JOAN *looks up, terrified.*)

BABA. It's an idea, sir.
FREDDIE. No. But seriously, we really ought to oil her joints or change her plugs or something.

(*He exits* L. BABA *picks up* FREDDIE'S *coat and* JOAN'S *dress, moves to the wardrobe up* C., *opens it, takes out two coat hangers, places the coat and dress on them, and then hangs them in the wardrobe.*)

BABA (*moving to the door* L. *and calling*). Are you ready for your bath, sir?
FREDDIE (*off; calling*). Yes.
BABA. Then take your trousers off this time, sir.
FREDDIE (*off; calling*). I generally do.

(*Without actually appearing,* FREDDIE *throws his trousers through the door* L. *to* BABA, *who catches them, moves up* C. *and hangs them in the wardrobe. He then moves to the table in the alcove, picks up a bottle of wine and moves with it to the dressing-table.* LADY GEVIPHIE *enters up* L.)

LADY GEVIPHIE. Ramshead.

(BABA *turns, startled.*)

Ramshead, is it you?
BABA. Is it? Yes. (*He looks in the dressing-table mirror.*) Yes, it is.
LADY GEVIPHIE. What are you doing here?
BABA. I am minding my own business, my lady.
LADY GEVIPHIE. Is this your room?
BABA. Well, it is the room I happen to be occupying temporarily.
LADY GEVIPHIE (*moving* C.). And where is my nephew?
BABA. Your which?

LADY GEVIPHIE. Where is Mr Frederick?

(BABA *moves* L. *of the bed and endeavours to place himself so that* LADY GEVIPHIE *cannot see* JOAN.)

Ah! (*She moves below the bed.*) There he is. (*She pulls down the coverlet and sees* JOAN.) Who is this creature?

BABA. That?

LADY GEVIPHIE. That.

BABA (*recovering his wits*). That is Mrs Ramshead.

LADY GEVIPHIE. Mrs Fiddlesticks.

BABA. I never fiddle. That is my spouse. One of the best spice of the species, if I may say so.

LADY GEVIPHIE. You know you don't possess a spouse.

BABA. Please, I've just pointed out to you. There she is.

LADY GEVIPHIE. Nonsense. I've known you for thirty years, and you've never had the vestige of a wife.

BABA. It's just one of those things that happen, my lady. You know, my lady, it's not a hereditary complaint, it's what you might call contractual. I mean, supposing you've never been run over and then suddenly you are. You can't say you're not run over, because you've never been before, can you? (*He moves* L., *rather proud of himself.*) That's pretty good, isn't it? (*He places the bottle of wine on the table* L.C.)

LADY GEVIPHIE. Are you asking me to believe that you have just married this creature?

BABA. Yes, but don't call her a creature, please. After all, we're all creatures.

LADY GEVIPHIE. Ramshead, you flatter yourself.

BABA. May I point out to you, my lady, that I am no longer in your employment, I have stuck on my last stamp for you.

LADY GEVIPHIE. And you certainly will not be in my employment again.

BABA. Which enables me to enquire, what right you have to come stalking into my bedroom—our bedroom—and interfering in my domestic affairs, right in the middle of my nuptials.

LADY GEVIPHIE. How dare you?

BABA. And how dare you poke your nose into my nuptials?

LADY GEVIPHIE. Ramshead.

BABA (*moving up* C.). I don't like anyone poking their nose into my nuptials, and I must ask you to go. (*He absent-mindedly opens the wardrobe door, mistaking it for the door up* L.)

(LADY GEVIPHIE *does not move.*)

Very well, if you won't, I shall ring up Whitehall one-two-one-two, and have you thrown out. (*He closes the wardrobe door and crosses* LADY GEVIPHIE *to the telephone.*)

LADY GEVIPHIE. Ramshead, don't be absurd. Put that telephone down.

BABA. Not while your nose remains in my nuptials.
LADY GEVIPHIE (*crossing to the armchair* L.C.). I shall not stir from this room until you tell me where Mr Frederick is. (*She sits.*)
BABA. Mr Freddie? I don't know where Mr Freddie is. She doesn't know either.
LADY GEVIPHIE. D'you expect me to believe that cock-and-bull story?
BABA. I shall be very disappointed if you don't—the bull part of it. (*He eases* C.) Listen, my lady, listen. First of all, you come barging into my room, sit there like the Queen of Sheba, and have the audacity to impugn my veracity. I will not have my veracity impugned (*he wags his finger at her*) with impunity.
LADY GEVIPHIE. Poppycock! He's in this hotel.
BABA. Possibly, possibly. I haven't engaged the whole hotel, but I have engaged this room, and I'm surprised that a lady of your presence, your prominence, should push her way into my private precincts, nose into my nuptials. (*Aside.*) I wonder what these nuptials are? (*He eases* R.)
LADY GEVIPHIE. They told me downstairs he was in room two nine—or was it nine two?
BABA. Ah, was it?
LADY GEVIPHIE. I'm not quite sure.
BABA. Then I suggest you go and find out.
LADY GEVIPHIE (*rising*). Very well, Ramshead, I may have made a mistake in the number. I apologize, but I still think you know where he is.
BABA. I do not.
LADY GEVIPHIE. You're quite sure, Ramshead?
BABA. May I die on this spot. (*He reacts, looks at the floor and hastily moves a step to* R.)
LADY GEVIPHIE. All right, I will try number ninety-two. (*She moves to the foot of the bed. To* JOAN.) Good night, madam. (*She turns and moves to the alcove up* L.)

(BABA *moves up* C., *rubbing his hands.*)

(*She turns and sees* BABA'S *glee.*) But remember—I'll be back.
BABA. I'll be glad to see your back—er—you back, my lady.

(*As* LADY GEVIPHIE *turns to the door,* FREDDIE *is heard calling off* L.)

FREDDIE (*off; calling*). Baba.
LADY GEVIPHIE (*turning sharply*). What's that?
BABA. What's what?
FREDDIE (*off; calling*). Baba.
LADY GEVIPHIE (*moving down* L.C.). That voice.

(BABA *crosses quickly to the table* L.C., *and picks up the bottle of wine.*)

BABA (*moving to the door up* L.). Baba, Baba—that's one of the sheep I count myself to sleep with at night. Good night.

(*He exits up* L. *As he does so,* FREDDIE, *minus his trousers, and with his shirt outside his pants, and still wearing shoes, socks, suspenders, collar and tie, enters hurriedly* L.)

FREDDIE (*as he enters*). Baba, you fool—you forgot to put the plug in the bath. (*He suddenly sees* LADY GEVIPHIE.) Ahhhh!
LADY GEVIPHIE. What does this mean? What are you doing here?
FREDDIE. I—er—I was having a kind of a bath, Auntie.
LADY GEVIPHIE. A kind of a bath, Freddie?
FREDDIE. Yes. You know—with soap, water, bubbles. You must have had one, Auntie.
LADY GEVIPHIE. Are you living here?
FREDDIE. In a kind of way, yes I am.
LADY GEVIPHIE. How could you?
FREDDIE. Well, you cut me off, Auntie. I've got to live somewhere.
LADY GEVIPHIE. You needn't talk as though I were the Gas Company. I see you don't want my company—you prefer the company of a discharged servant. The whole thing is a conspiracy between you and Ramshead. Well, I don't wish to have anything to do with him—but you, Freddie? How could you do such a thing?
FREDDIE. What have I done?
LADY GEVIPHIE (*indicating* JOAN). What is she doing in your bed?
FREDDIE. She's not doing anything at the moment, is she?
LADY GEVIPHIE. Who is she?
FREDDIE. Oh, that's nothing, Auntie. It's just someone I take around and sleep with. Honestly.
LADY GEVIPHIE. Are you married to her?
FREDDIE. Married? Oh, Lord, no. Only pretending to be.
LADY GEVIPHIE. Pretending? But that's worse.
FREDDIE. Well, Auntie, I had to earn a living somehow.
LADY GEVIPHIE. Freddie, do you mean to say she pays you to do it?
FREDDIE. No, she doesn't. The man who owns her—he does. (*He crosses* R., *below the bed.*) Mark you, he's quite capable of doing the job himself, only he wants an outside opinion on what she can do, so he pays me to take her around, that's all.
LADY GEVIPHIE. I can hardly believe my ears. I've never been so shocked in all my life. You take money from this man . . .
FREDDIE. Auntie, I'm sorry. I've let you get the wrong end of the stick. (*He laughs.*) You didn't think she was a real lady, did you?
LADY GEVIPHIE. I certainly did not.
FREDDIE. Oh, that's fine, then you understand. Mind, she's very well made. (*He moves to the bed, turns back the bedclothes and reveals all of* JOAN.)

(LADY GEVIPHIE *turns her back to the bed.*)

LADY GEVIPHIE. I'll take your word for it. I've no doubt you know all about that by now.
FREDDIE. Well, good heavens, I ought to. I've tested her out in every way. Auntie, her movements, you wouldn't believe it. Nothing mechanical about them at all. Look at this figure—I'll show you how she works if you like.
LADY GEVIPHIE. No, thank you.
FREDDIE. The Professor calls her Robert, or something.
LADY GEVIPHIE. Robert?
FREDDIE. You know, mechanical figure—works by wireless.
LADY GEVIPHIE. You mean a robot?
FREDDIE. Yes, that's it. It's made of plastic or rubber or something. I don't know what it's made of, but look at the result. Isn't it terrific?
LADY GEVIPHIE (*turning*). Are you implying that this isn't a real woman at all?
FREDDIE. Auntie, I'm telling you, it's a robot, a figure.
LADY GEVIPHIE. So that is your explanation?
FREDDIE. Yes, please, Auntie.
LADY GEVIPHIE. I see. (*She moves to the door up* L.) I never want to see your face again.
FREDDIE (*re-covering* JOAN). My face? What's my face got to do with it?
LADY GEVIPHIE (*moving to the foot of the bed*). It's bad enough to find you leading this dissolute life—to listen to your lies—but when on top of that, you insult my intelligence by . . .
FREDDIE. But, Auntie, I swear it.
LADY GEVIPHIE. You still insist that that is not a real woman?
FREDDIE. No. No part of her's real. She can't think. She can't see, she can't hear, she can't feel. She's a robot, a figure.
LADY GEVIPHIE (*taking a brooch from her dress*). You say she can't feel, eh?
FREDDIE. No, not a thing.

(LADY GEVIPHIE *moves above the bed, pulls the covers down, and stabs* JOAN *with a pin.* JOAN *screams loudly, sits up and starts to cry.* LADY GEVIPHIE *moves* L. *of the bed.*)

LADY GEVIPHIE. Can't feel a thing. Casanova.

(*She turns, sweeps to the door up* L., *and exits.* FREDDIE *runs to the door after her, panic stricken.*)

FREDDIE (*calling*). Auntie, Auntie. Come back. (*He hesitates, looks at* JOAN *and cannot make up his mind what to do. He finally moves to the foot of the bed, and knocks shyly on the suitcase. He is unconscious of his own state of undress.*) Good evening.
JOAN (*sobbing*). Good evening.
FREDDIE (*moving quickly to the dressing-table and straightening his*

tie in the mirror). The name is Cavendish. I—er—I don't think I've had the—er—pleasure . . .
JOAN. I'm Joan.
FREDDIE (*easing above the foot of the bed*). Oh, yes. J-Joan. How do you do ?
JOAN. Not awfully well, thank you.
FREDDIE. Oh, no, I don't suppose so.
JOAN. I hate your aunt.
FREDDIE. I hate her, too, as a matter of fact. And she does not seem to be very fond of you, does she ? But tell me—how does all this come about ? I mean, what are we—sort of—doing here ?
JOAN. It was only a joke.
FREDDIE. Oh, a joke. I see. Quite a funny one, too, isn't it ?
JOAN. It was only because my uncle wouldn't let me go out anywhere. And then I heard him telling you about the robot, and you saying that you would take it out—and I thought it would be fun to pretend that I was the robot and let you take me.
FREDDIE. Ahhhh ! (*He sits on the upstage side of the bed.*) Then you are not the robot, at all ?
JOAN. No, I'm Joan.
FREDDIE. Yes, yes, I've got that. I'm just trying to keep sane, that's all. But there is a robot ?
JOAN. Yes. Uncle made it. But I hid it—and took its place. I only wanted an evening out—and a bit of fun.
FREDDIE. I know just how you feel, and by Jove, you've certainly had it, haven't you ?
JOAN. It's been horrid—and very painful. (*She rubs herself.*)
FREDDIE. Oh, I'm so sorry. Can I give it a rub ?
JOAN. No.
FREDDIE. I keep forgetting that you're not the robot. Why didn't you tell me before ?
JOAN. I was afraid that you'd be cross.
FREDDIE (*horrified at the idea*). Me ? Cross with you ?
JOAN. Well, I didn't know what you might do to me.
FREDDIE. I couldn't have done anything much worse than I have done, could I ?
JOAN. I don't know.
FREDDIE. I see what you mean.
JOAN. I'm very sorry, Mr Cavendish.
FREDDIE. Call me Freddie.
JOAN. Freddie.
FREDDIE. I say, we have sort of got together, haven't we ? I'm glad about that—say that you're glad, too.
JOAN. Well, perhaps—just a little.
FREDDIE. Oh, that's marvellous, isn't it ? Well, we're all off on the right foot now, aren't we ? Well, what do we do now ?
JOAN. I'm going to get dressed.
FREDDIE. Yes, yes. That's a good idea. You really ought not

to go about like that, you might catch cold. (*He slaps his own knees and belatedly notices that he has no trousers on. He rises hurriedly, moves to the wardrobe, takes out* JOAN's *dress, throws it over the end of the bed and then takes his own suit from the wardrobe.*)

(*Endeavouring all the time to hold his shirt down to cover his legs, he backs to the door* L. *and exits.*)

JOAN (*getting out of the bed ; calling*). Freddie.
FREDDIE (*off ; calling*). Yes?
JOAN (*proceeding to put on her dress*). Will you take me home?
FREDDIE. Well—when I've got my trousers on.
JOAN. I meant when you'd—when you were fully dressed.
FREDDIE. You bet I will. I say . . .
JOAN. Yes.
FREDDIE. What's your uncle going to say about this?
JOAN. I don't know.
FREDDIE. I don't think he's going to be very pleased, you know.
JOAN (*moving to the dressing-table and adjusting her hair*). I won't tell him. He won't be home till eleven, I know, so we must get the real robot here before he gets back.
FREDDIE. Oh, is that necessary?
JOAN. Well, if you want to earn that money.
FREDDIE. Oh, the money. D'you know, I'd forgotten all about the money. I say?
JOAN. Yes?
FREDDIE. Do you think I'll like her?
JOAN (*moving* C.). That depends on your taste.
FREDDIE. Is she anything like you?
JOAN. Uncle thinks she's the perfect woman.

(FREDDIE, *now fully dressed, enters* L.)

FREDDIE (*as he enters*). Oh, does he? Well, I think you are. Do you really want me to fetch this other thing back here?
JOAN. Of course.
FREDDIE. But why?
JOAN. Well—it'll give us a chance to meet again.
FREDDIE. Oh, I never thought of that.
JOAN. What about your aunt?
FREDDIE. Oh, she'll love you when she gets to know you.

(JOAN *rubs herself ruefully.*)

It's only that she doesn't like anything unconventional, that's all. Anyway, this is only for a week, and I expect the robot'll remind me of you.
JOAN (*laughing*). You wait till you see her.
FREDDIE (*heroically*). Well, I'll do it because of you.
JOAN (*turning her back to* FREDDIE *for him to fasten her dress*). Do you mind?

ACT II]   THE PERFECT WOMAN   53

FREDDIE (*absently*). Not at all. (*He realizes what she wants.*) Not at all, I'm sorry. (*He fastens her dress.*)
JOAN. Goodness, I look an awful mess. (*She rubs herself again.*) Ooh!
FREDDIE. What's the matter?
JOAN. That horrid woman stuck that pin right in me.
FREDDIE. Does it hurt?
JOAN. Yes, it does.
FREDDIE (*lifting her dress*). Let's have a look.
JOAN (*moving away sharply*). No.
FREDDIE. Oh, sorry. I keep forgetting you're real.
JOAN (*moving in R. of* FREDDIE *and looking into his face*). Do you?
FREDDIE (*moving close to her*). Well—not really. (*He kisses her.*) You're real. Come on.

(*He takes her by the hand and they move quickly to the door up L. As they reach it,* BABA *enters up L. and they bump into him.* BABA *is carrying a bottle and is slightly drunk.*)

Good night, Baba.
JOAN (*playfully slapping* BABA'S *face*). Good night, Baba.

(FREDDIE *and* JOAN *exit up L.*)

BABA (*moving unsteadily* C.). It talks.

CURTAIN.

ACT III

SCENE.—*The same as Act II. 10 p.m. the same evening.*

When the CURTAIN *rises, the stage is in darkness except for the bedside lamp.* BABA, *wearing shirt, trousers, shoes and his hat, is sitting up in bed, reading a magazine, which is upside down. There is an empty bottle on the bedside cabinet. After a few moments he realizes the magazine is upside down and as he turns it, he notices the bottle, which he picks up. He raises it to his lips, discovers that it is empty, throws it on the floor and resumes reading.* LADY GEVIPHIE *enters up* L.)

LADY GEVIPHIE *(as she enters)*. Freddie. Freddie. *(She switches on the lights and sees* BABA.) Ramshead.

BABA. Hail Titania. *(He raises his hat.)* Goodmorrow, sweet sooth.

LADY GEVIPHIE *(moving to the foot of the bed)*. Ramshead, where is Mr Freddie?

BABA. Ah! Where is he?

LADY GEVIPHIE. Where has he gone?

BABA. If I knew where he'd gone, I'd know where he is—where is he?

LADY GEVIPHIE. I left him here an hour ago.

BABA. S'mistake. Shouldn't have done it—can't leave anything around these days. Bounda get lost.

LADY GEVIPHIE *(moving above the bed to* BABA *and shaking his left shoulder)*. Ramshead, will you pull yourself together and listen to me? He had that female with him.

BABA. Lucky fellow.

LADY GEVIPHIE. What has he done with her?

BABA. I'm a little too young to know, my lady.

LADY GEVIPHIE *(moving to the foot of the bed)*. Well, I must find him. He is still my nephew and I'm responsible for him. Ramshead...

BABA *(raising his hat)*. Mr Ramshead to you, my lady.

LADY GEVIPHIE. Drunk again.

BABA. Are you? Oh dear, dear, dear.

LADY GEVIPHIE. T'cha. Ramshead, I'm certain he's hiding here somewhere, and I intend to find him. *(She moves to the door* L., *opens it, looks off, closes the door and turns.)* He's not there.

(BABA *leans out of bed, opens the cupboard of the bedside cabinet, peers in, then closes the door hurriedly.)*

(Exasperated.) Ohhh!

ACT III]   THE PERFECT WOMAN   55

BABA. And nothing up my sleeve.
LADY GEVIPHIE (*moving to the wardrobe*). And absolutely nothing under your hat. (*She looks in the wardrobe.*)
BABA. My lady, I mus' again point out that it is unsleep—un—seem—ly for you to be in my room—middle of the night. Poking your nose into my nuptials. (*He pauses.*) Where've I heard that before? May I remind you that I have a character to lose, my good woman.
LADY GEVIPHIE (*moving* C.). I am not your good woman.
BABA. Oh. Well, even if you haven't a character to lose, I have, my—woman. And if anybody should come—catch you and me together here, my room—whoo! What's the answer? Animal, vegetable, or municipal?
LADY GEVIPHIE. I see through your little game, Ramshead. You know exactly where my nephew is. Well, if I have to search every room in this hotel I'll find him and save him from that woman. And as for you, Ramshead . . .
RAMSHEAD (*raising his hat*). *Mr* Ramshead to you, my lady. (*He looks vacantly at his hat, then leans out of the bed and puts the hat in the bedside cupboard.*)
LADY GEVIPHIE (*moving up* L.). Oh! Don't forget—(*she turns.*)
BABA
LADY GEVIPHIE } (*together*). I'll be back.

(LADY GEVIPHIE *exits angrily up* L.)

BABA (*calling*). Put the light out. Put the . . . Oh, she's gone. Have to do it myself, I suppose. Have to do everything myself. (*He looks around.*) Ooh, lost me hat. (*He gets out of the bed, blows at the bedside lamp and switches it out, then looks vacantly around the room.*) Where's the switch, can't find the switch—oh, yes. (*He moves unsteadily to the door up* L., *finds the switch and turns out all the remaining lights.*) Oh—dark, can't find the bed. (*He fumbles around the room.*) Los' the bed, mus' ring up Winkel, ask him to send another bed. (*He finds his way to the bedside cabinet, switches on the lamp, sits on the downstage edge of the bed, lifts the telephone receiver and speaks into it.*) Hello, is that Cockle Cockle—oh, Winkel. Tell him I want him up here—I've lost my hat . . . Wha' number? . . . The number is . . . (*He compares the telephone dial with his wrist watch.*) Your clock's fast, isn't it? . . . Oh, the number, hol' the line. (*He puts the receiver down, rises, moves to the door up* L., *opens it, looks at the number, and moves to the telephone, muttering.*) Twenty-nine, twenty-nine, twenty-nine. (*He picks up the receiver and speaks into it.*) Hello, the number is . . . I've forgotten it. Wait a minute. (*He puts the receiver down, crosses and looks at the door* L.) They've rubbed it out. (*He turns and sees the number on the door up* L., *crosses to the telephone, lifts the receiver and speaks into it.*) Hello—it's twenty-nine . . . I said twenty-nine . . . Well, if you knew it was twenty-nine, what did you want to make me traipse all over the hotel for . . . ? Where's Winkel?

(WINKEL *enters quietly up* L.)

(*Into the telephone. Angrily.*) Hello.
 WINKEL. Hello.
 BABA (*still into the telephone*). Hello.
 WINKEL. Hello.
 BABA (*taking his hat out of the cabinet*). Don't keep saying "hello". (*He puts his hat on.*) I told them to send you up here, in number twenty-nine.
 WINKEL. I am here, sir.
 BABA. I don't want you there—I want you here in number twenty-nine.
 WINKEL. Yes, sir.
 BABA. Listen. I've lost my hat.
 WINKEL. It's on your head, sir.
 BABA. Don't be ridiculous. If it was on my head I'd . . . (*He feels his head and discovers his hat.*) So it is.
 WINKEL. I can see it, sir.
 BABA. You can see it? (*He looks into the mouthpiece of the receiver, then turns and sees* WINKEL *for the first time.*) Ah, Winkel, get out of here and fetch me a drink. (*He replaces the receiver.*)
 WINKEL. Yes, sir.

(*He exits hurriedly up* L. BABA *takes off his hat, puts it on the cabinet, gets into the bed and pulls the coverlet up over him.* FREDDIE *enters up* L. *and switches on the lights.*)

FREDDIE (*looking off up* L.). Walk.

(*The real* ROBOT *enters up* L. *in a rather mechanical manner. It is a rather horrid looking thing, dressed in a prison-shaped black dress.*)

Stop.

(*The* ROBOT *stops.*)

Right.

(*The* ROBOT *faces the audience.*)

Walk.

(*The* ROBOT *moves down* C.)

Stop.

(*The* ROBOT *stops* C.)

BABA (*peering out from under the covers*). Put that light out. (*He sees the* ROBOT. (*He dives back under the covers.*)
 FREDDIE (*moving* L. *of the bed*). Baba. What are you doing there? Come out of there, Baba.

ACT III]   THE PERFECT WOMAN   57

BABA (*sitting up*). Send your aunt away and I'll talk to you.
FREDDIE. That's not my aunt, it's the robot.
BABA. What?
FREDDIE. The robot.
BABA. What is?
FREDDIE. That.
BABA. Who is it?
FREDDIE. I keep telling you. It's her—the robot. The figure.
BABA. What have you done to her?
FREDDIE. Nothing. It isn't the one we had here before. I took her home. She's real—not a robot at all.
BABA. Well, take her home, too.
FREDDIE. What the deuce is the matter with you, Baba? (*He sniffs.*) Oh, what a terrible smell of trifle. Listen—I brought her here.
BABA. Whaffor?
FREDDIE. To sleep.
BABA. Where?
FREDDIE (*indicating the bed*). There.
BABA (*hastily getting out of the bed*). Not with me.
FREDDIE. Of course not with you. What were you doing in that bed, anyway? You've no right to be there at all.

(*The* ROBOT *turns and faces* R.)

BABA. No right?

(*The* ROBOT *turns and faces up stage.*)

I have every right.

(*The* ROBOT *turns and faces* L.)

FREDDIE. Oh, stop saying it. She keeps doing it.
BABA. I like that. That's good. Who is this woman?
FREDDIE. Baba, you're tight. I keep telling you that this is the robot woman that we have to take for a walk. Right?

(*The* ROBOT *moves* L., *turns and walks towards the footlights.*)

(*To the* ROBOT.) Oh! Stop. (*He takes* BABA *by the arm and leads him to the door* L.) Come along, Baba, I'm going to put your head under the tap and leave it there until you're sober.
BABA (*to the* ROBOT). Good-bye, streetcar.

(FREDDIE *and* BABA *exit* L. WINKEL, *carrying a bottle in each hand, enters up* L. *He sees the* ROBOT, *thinks he is in the wrong room, turns, looks at the number on the door up* L., *then moves down to* L. *of the* ROBOT.)

WINKEL (*to the* ROBOT). The sir. He want another drink. Where is the sir? Do you want the booze? Oh, I see. Do you know where is the sir? Has he left?

(*The* ROBOT *turns and faces* WINKEL.)

Is it that to you I also must not talk ? Is he of you too yallous ?—I understand. You know it not where he is ?—perhaps he has gone for a walk.

(*The* ROBOT *starts to walk straight at* WINKEL, *who backs away, muttering in German and dodges aside as the* ROBOT *moves to the door* L. *and exits. There is the sound of some confusion off* L., *then* BABA *enters hurriedly and collides with* WINKEL. *They look at each other, panic stricken, then turn, move quickly to the door up* L. *and exit hurriedly.*)

FREDDIE (*off*). Walk.

(*The* ROBOT, *followed by* FREDDIE, *enters* L. *When the* ROBOT *reaches a position below the bed*, FREDDIE *calls.*)

Stop.
                (*The* ROBOT *stops below the bed.*)

Left.
                (*The* ROBOT *turns and faces the audience.*)

(*He crosses to* L. *of the* ROBOT.) Now, Duckie, I'm going to get you into bed. (*He undoes her dress at the back, and slips it to the floor.*) More poppers.

(*The* ROBOT'S *undergarment is composed of plastic and has several dials and pieces of wire on it.*)

If you think I'm enjoying this, you're mistaken. Step back.

(*The* ROBOT *steps back to the downstage edge of the bed. He picks up the dress and throws it over the foot of the bed. He moves to her and twirls one of the dials.*)

Never can get the Third Programme. Now I'm going to get you into bed. (*He tries to push her into the bed, but at first cannot move her.*) Oh, so you want to play rough, think you're tough, eh ? Well, here goes. (*He stands close to her, facing her, gives a big heave and gets her on to the bed.*)

(*The* ROBOT *sits on the edge of the bed. She only bends at the hips, so that her legs, sticking straight out, come up between* FREDDIE'S *and kick him.*)

(*He moves to the doors up* L.) I'm going to close that door. I don't want anybody to see what I'm going to bed with. (*He closes the door, moves above the bed, leans over and pulls the* ROBOT *round to a sitting position on it.*)

(*He pushes her so that her back is on the bed but her legs are in the air. He presses her legs down and she sits up again. He pushes her body down and her legs come up once more. He tries to get her legs straightened out and presses one down, but as he takes the other, the first flies up and his head is caught between her feet. He frees himself, but the* ROBOT *is still in a bent position, with her feet in the air.*)

There must be a gadget to straighten this out. (*He presses a switch in the* ROBOT'S *middle.*)

(*The* ROBOT *straightens out.*)

Phew ! Well, you're in, you horror. (*He pulls the coverlet over her and moves below the bed.*) I'm only taking my coat off if I've got to sleep with a flying fortress. (*He removes his coat and places it on the chair down* R.) Well, give me some room. Turn left.

(*The* ROBOT *rolls over on its side.*)

That's better. Good night, *dear.*

(*He settles down, and is about to switch off the bedside lamp when* FARINI *enters up* L.)

FARINI. Mr Cavendish, I do not wish to disturb you on your wedding night . . .
FREDDIE (*sitting up*). What do you want ?
FARINI. It's all right, sir.

(*The* ROBOT *turns on her back.*)

Don't get up.

(*The* ROBOT *sits up.*)

(*He eases* C. *To the* ROBOT.) Good evening. (*Startled.*) Ah ! Mr Cavendish. What is this ?
FREDDIE. It's nothing. (*To the* ROBOT.) Lie down.

(*The* ROBOT *lies down.*)

You don't understand, Farini.
FARINI. Mr Cavendish, I try hard to understand the English wedding night . . .
FREDDIE. What do you mean ?
FARINI. Sir, I understand the best man in the bath—but the mother-in-law in the bed—I no understand.
FREDDIE (*getting out of the bed*). Farini, are you insinuating anything ? (*He picks up his coat and puts it on.*)
FARINI. Mr Cavendish, I am a man of the world and above all I am a brass monkey—I see all, hear all and say nothing. (*He moves up* L.) Good night, Mr Cavendish.

(LADY GEVIPHIE *enters up* L.)

(*He looks at* LADY GEVIPHIE *in astonishment.*) My God, another bridesmaid.

(*He exits up* L.)

LADY GEVIPHIE (*moving* C.). Freddie. There you are.
FREDDIE (*moving* L. *of the bed*). Yes, Auntie, here I are.
LADY GEVIPHIE. Of course he lied to me.
FREDDIE. Who did?
LADY GEVIPHIE. That worm, Ramshead.
FREDDIE. Oh, yes, he would. He wouldn't lie to some people, but he would lie to you.
LADY GEVIPHIE. Where have you been?
FREDDIE (*confused*). Auntie, where haven't I been.
LADY GEVIPHIE. Where's that girl you had here?
FREDDIE. I took her home. That's where I've been—taking her home.
LADY GEVIPHIE. I'm very glad to hear it. And now you're coming home with me.
FREDDIE. With you, Auntie? But I can't do that. You cut me off.
LADY GEVIPHIE. No, Freddie, I've decided to forgive you.
FREDDIE. What, again?
LADY GEVIPHIE. Yes, dear. I am responsible for you, so you can come back with me now and I'll help you to turn over a new leaf.
FREDDIE. I've got some old leaves to turn back first, Auntie. I mean, I can't leave here. I've got to stay around, Auntie.
LADY GEVIPHIE. Why?
FREDDIE. I have other commitments. There are others dependent on me.
LADY GEVIPHIE. What others?
FREDDIE. Well, actually, it's only one.
LADY GEVIPHIE. I thought so. That wretched ex-butler of mine.
FREDDIE. No, it isn't.
LADY GEVIPHIE. I don't want to hear another word about him, Freddie—he's done you quite enough harm already. Come along, dear.
FREDDIE. No, Auntie, you're mistaken.
LADY GEVIPHIE. I'm not mistaken about that fellow's character. He is the most degraded, dissolute, debased, degenerate, dissipated, debauched . . .
FREDDIE. Oh, Auntie, what a lot of D's you know.
LADY GEVIPHIE. I've already had two interviews with him this evening, and although I have no desire for a third . . .
FREDDIE (*interrupting*). Can we discuss this downstairs?
LADY GEVIPHIE. Certainly not. (*She tries to peer past* FREDDIE *to see who is in the bed.*) I wish him to understand thoroughly . . .
FREDDIE. Can I say one word?
LADY GEVIPHIE. Certainly not.
FREDDIE. Can I say half a word?
LADY GEVIPHIE. Certainly not. If he thinks he can gain any-

thing through you ... (*She slips past* FREDDIE, *moves above the bed and pulls off the covers.*) Do you understand that, you ... (*She sees the* ROBOT.) Ah! What, another? (*She moves* C.) Freddie, what is the meaning of this?
FREDDIE. Auntie, you've had your twenty questions.
LADY GEVIPHIE. Are you a Mormon?
FREDDIE. I'm not even a Mason. I think I'm a seventh-day adventurer.
LADY GEVIPHIE. Looks very much like it to me. You told me that you'd taken that girl home, but you didn't tell me that you'd brought another one here. Old leaves indeed.
FREDDIE. Don't call her that, the Professor might not like it.
LADY GEVIPHIE. What Professor?
FREDDIE. The Professor who made her.
LADY GEVIPHIE. Are you trying to tell me that absurd story again?
FREDDIE. I'm not trying to, Auntie, you're dragging it out of me.
LADY GEVIPHIE. You want me to believe that this one isn't a real woman either—is that it?
FREDDIE. Auntie, I want you to believe just that.
LADY GEVIPHIE. I'm not quite such a fool as I look.
FREDDIE. I don't see how you could be.
LADY GEVIPHIE. What?
FREDDIE. I mean—oh, you twist everything round.
LADY GEVIPHIE (*to the* ROBOT). You horrible creature, sit up.

(*The* ROBOT *sits up.*)

Not real, eh?
FREDDIE. Oh, she can do that. She can do anything she's told. (*To the* ROBOT.) Lie down.

(*The* ROBOT *lies down.*)

You see, it's a robot, a figure. She cannot think, she cannot see, she cannot hear, she cannot feel. Oh, I've said all this before tonight.
LADY GEVIPHIE (*taking a brooch from her dress*). Oh, this one can't feel either? (*She moves above the bed.*)
FREDDIE. Now, Auntie, don't try any of your silly tricks, you'll be sorry ...
LADY GEVIPHIE (*jabbing the pin into the* ROBOT). Oh! (*She starts back, clasping her hand.*)
FREDDIE. There you are, short circuit—serves you right.
LADY GEVIPHIE (*moving* C.). Well, either she has iron self-control or she wears steel corsets.
FREDDIE. Rather, armour-plated. (*He attempts to demonstrate on* LADY GEVIPHIE'S *chest.*) She's got fore and aft shock absorbers, (*he realizes what he is doing in time*) and a dashboard, with gadgets on it.

LADY GEVIPHIE (*taking hold of* FREDDIE'S *left arm and leading him down* C.). Freddie, I believe I've misjudged you after all. Now tell me the truth about this.
FREDDIE. Auntie, I'm trying to tell you. It's the Professor.
LADY GEVIPHIE. What Professor?
FREDDIE. Professor Belmon, the man who made her.
LADY GEVIPHIE. Not *the* Professor Belmon?
FREDDIE. The Professor Belmon, as ever was.
LADY GEVIPHIE. Not Professor Archibald Belmon?
FREDDIE. I don't know whether he's bald or not, dear. But his name's Belmon. D'you know him, Auntie?
LADY GEVIPHIE. Well, yes, actually I did know Archie—er—Professor Belmon, rather well. He was a slim dapper man with a dear little dark moustache.
FREDDIE. Well, something terrible's happened to him since then.
LADY GEVIPHIE. Actually, he was very fond of me. Of course, he was much older than I was. (*She turns away. Girlishly.*) Heigh-ho.
FREDDIE. The wind and the rain. Yes, well, I thought he was a friend of mine till he launched that battleship on me.
LADY GEVIPHIE. Well, what are we going to do with it?
FREDDIE. I've got to take it about with me or I don't get the money.
LADY GEVIPHIE. Fiddlededee.
FREDDIE. Oh, fiddle-me-foot—all right—de-dee.
LADY GEVIPHIE (*moving to* FREDDIE). Don't be so naughty. (*She slaps his hand.*) I won't have you making such a fool of yourself. We must take it back to Professor Belmon at once.
FREDDIE. How can I? I haven't tried it out yet.
LADY GEVIPHIE. Don't argue with me. Get that thing out of bed.
FREDDIE. Oh, all right. (*He moves below the bed. To the* ROBOT.) You've got to get up. Auntie's here. (*Savagely.*) Sit up.

(*The* ROBOT *sits up.*)

Right.

(*The* ROBOT *swings her legs off the bed and sits facing the audience with her legs straight out in front.*)

Stand up.

(*The* ROBOT *rises.*)

(*To* LADY GEVIPHIE.) It is real, isn't it?
LADY GEVIPHIE. Uncanny.
FREDDIE (*moving and picking up the dress*). She's uncanny all right.
LADY GEVIPHIE. Can it dress itself?
FREDDIE (*moving* R. *of the* ROBOT). No, I have to be its nursemaid and everything. It's an awful job. (*He bends down.*) I think I'll

try this end this time. (*He holds the dress ready. To the* ROBOT.) Step in.

(*The* ROBOT *takes a step forward, but not into the dress.*)

No. Step in.

(*The* ROBOT *takes another step forward, but still not into the dress.*)

No, don't be dumb. (*He bends over, holding the dress.*) Lift your knee.

(*The* ROBOT *lifts her knee and bangs him under the chin.*)

Ooh! She's doing it on purpose, you know. She's really quite intelligent. She's just being nasty now.

LADY GEVIPHIE. Put it over her head. Here, give it to me.

(FREDDIE *gives* LADY GEVIPHIE *the dress.*)

Now, make her put her arms up.

(*The* ROBOT *puts her arms up suddenly, nearly knocking* LADY GEVIPHIE *over.*)

FREDDIE. Auntie, will you stop giving her orders?
LADY GEVIPHIE (*finding she cannot reach*). Bring me a chair.

(FREDDIE *moves the chair from down* R. *to down* R. *of the* ROBOT.)

FREDDIE. Are you going up on this?

(*He helps* LADY GEVIPHIE *up on to the chair.*)

LADY GEVIPHIE. Don't let me fall.
FREDDIE. Famous last words. I've got you, Auntie. They ought to get a building licence to erect something as big as you, Auntie.
LADY GEVIPHIE (*putting the dress over the* ROBOT'S *arms and head*). Does the Professor dress this thing himself?
FREDDIE. I don't know, I've never seen him actually at it.
LADY GEVIPHIE. He's not much of a dress designer, is he?
FREDDIE. He probably bought the dress first and stuffed it afterwards, like a sausage.
LADY GEVIPHIE. She certainly has no figure.
FREDDIE (*looking pointedly at* LADY GEVIPHIE'S *figure*). Couldn't you spare her some of yours, Auntie?
LADY GEVIPHIE. Rude boy. (*She laughs.*) Help me down.

(FREDDIE *assists her down, and replaces the chair down* R.)

(*She straightens the* ROBOT'S *dress.*) There, how's that? (*She fastens the dress at the back.*)

FREDDIE (*moving to the* ROBOT *and adjusting the front of the dress*). Her steering wheel is in the correct position. Left. (*He moves to* LADY GEVIPHIE.)

(*The* ROBOT *turns and faces* L.)

She looks quite pretty if you close your eyes tightly.
LADY GEVIPHIE (*moving* L. *of the* ROBOT, *facing her and making an adjustment to the dress*). I was afraid that chair wasn't going to hold me.

(*The* ROBOT *puts her arms around* LADY GEVIPHIE *and holds her very tightly.*)

Ooh! Oh! Stop it.

(*She struggles to release herself.* FREDDIE *tries to help, but only succeeds in toppling them over so that* LADY GEVIPHIE *is flat on the floor and the* ROBOT *is over her in an arched position, hands and feet on the floor, but the rest of her bent up in the middle.*)

FREDDIE (*running to the door up* L. *and calling excitedly*). It's the Robot, it's attacking my auntie. Help. Help. (*He turns, moves above the* ROBOT, *tries to pull her off and then crawls underneath her and tries to lift her.*)

(*The* ROBOT *collapses and* FREDDIE *is caught between the* ROBOT *and* LADY GEVIPHIE. BABA *enters up* L.)

BABA (*facetiously*). Having a game with the girls?
FREDDIE (*shouting excitedly*). Don't be a fool. This thing weighs a ton. Get the Professor.
BABA (*moving down* R.). Who?
FREDDIE. The Professor.
BABA. Where is he?
FREDDIE. On the telephone.
BABA. Do you know his number off-hand?
FREDDIE. I don't know anything off-hand. Look in the book.
BABA (*moving to the bedside cabinet*). What's his name? (*He picks up the telephone directory.*)
FREDDIE. Belmon.
BABA (*looking in the directory*). How does he spell it?
FREDDIE. With a B—you B-fool.

(FARINI *enters up* L., *looks horror-struck, raises his hands, screams, turns and exits.* BABA *puts the telephone directory on the bed, moves above the group on the floor and drags* FREDDIE *out by the feet.*)

(*He rises, gasping.*) Baba, you've saved my life. (*He shakes* BABA *by the hand.*)
BABA. Don't mention it, sir.
FREDDIE. You have. I'll never forget you. Now we've got to save auntie.
BABA. Is that necessary, sir?
FREDDIE. Shurrup. Don't be callous. Baba, we must get the Professor and find out what the word is.
BABA. Open sesame.
FREDDIE. Shut up—they might do anything to that. (*He picks*

up the telephone directory and turns the pages.) Bass—Bass—Bass, what a lot of Bass. Berkshire, Berkeley, Bell, Belmon—got it. (*He puts the directory down, lifts the telephone receiver and dials a number.*)

(*There is a pause.*)

(*Into the telephone.*) Hello, Professor, thank heavens. It's me . . . Cavendish. Remember ? The blithering idiot who took that job of yours . . . What's wrong ? Everything's wrong. Your robot's attacked my auntie . . . Of course it matters . . . What's the word to disentangle her ? . . . Oh, of course. Hang on, Professor. (*He looks up.*) Baba.

BABA. Yes, sir ?

FREDDIE. I've got it. (*To the* ROBOT.) Ermyntrude, double-de-clutch.

(*The* ROBOT *rolls up stage on to her back.*)

BABA. Why didn't we think of this before ?

FREDDIE (*putting the receiver down and rising*). This is an emergency. Auntie, we could have de-clutched you ages ago. Help me, Baba, to get her up.

(*They lift* LADY GEVIPHIE *to her feet and then, holding her, push her back to the bed,* FREDDIE *shouting at her as though she was a horse.*)

Back, back—good girl. Come-on—wooooo.

(*They lay her on the bed and* FREDDIE *puts the coverlet over her.*)

Baba, I don't like the look of her.

BABA. I never did, sir. (*He pulls the coverlet over her face.*)

FREDDIE (*moving to the telephone, lifting the receiver and speaking into it.*) Professor, is Dr Jackson staying with you ? . . . Good . . . I think you ought to bring him round here . . . Well, get out of bed, it's me auntie.

(LADY GEVIPHIE *groans.*)

(*Dramatically.*) Professor, I think auntie's going . . . I said I think auntie's going . . . Where ? How should I know where ? . . . Oh, she's all right. (*He looks at the* ROBOT.) Ermyntrude, get up.

(*The* ROBOT, *accompanied by ratchet noises, heaves herself three times in the middle, but collapses each time.*)

BABA. Acute indigestion, if you ask me, sir.

FREDDIE (*to* BABA). Shut up. (*Into the telephone.*) That noise, Professor ? . . . (*To* BABA.) He's heard it. (*Into the telephone.*) No, Professor, to be quite truthful she's still lying down . . . What ? But you can't blame us . . . How much ? . . . Two thousand pounds. But, Professor, be reasonable . . . Professor . . . Profess . . . (*He rattles the receiver rest but gets no reply, and replaces the receiver.*) Baba, we're sunk. (*He rises.*)

BABA (*moving to the door up* L.). To the lifeboats, sir. Come along.

FREDDIE (*moving* C.). No, no. You've got to stand by me. The Professor's coming round here, and he says if we've broken his perfect woman, it'll cost two thousand pounds to build another.

BABA. Two thousand pounds, sir?

FREDDIE. Two thousand pounds for a lot of tin and wire. (*He sits on the luggage rack.*) Think of the delivery date—we'll never get a licence even.

BABA. Don't you know anything about electricity?

FREDDIE. I don't even know the difference between a dry battery and a wet one.

BABA. I once made a crystal set in the early days of wireless.

FREDDIE. Crystal set—you know what always went wrong with those.

BABA. Everything.

FREDDIE (*rising*). No, no—the cat's whisker.

(*They move and kneel above the* ROBOT. BABA *lifts her dress and they try to find something they can recognize.*)

Oh, it's no good—it's all modern stuff.

BABA. She may have blown a fuse.

FREDDIE. I can mend a fuse. Where's her fuse-box?

BABA. It's very often under the stairs.

FREDDIE. Oh—shut up.

(*They turn the* ROBOT *over, search her back for a fuse-box, then rise from their knees and survey her anxiously.*)

Ermyntrude—get up, please.

(*The* ROBOT *pushes her backside into the air three times to the accompaniment of rattle noises, but collapses each time.*)

BABA. Oh, I think she's doing the Lancers, sir.

FREDDIE. Oh, try and be serious for a minute, will you? Look, I've an idea, so let's get her out of sight into the bathroom before the Professor comes.

(*They each take one of the* ROBOT'S *arms, and dragging her between them, move to the door* L. *and exit. There is a few moments pause, then* BELMON, JACKSON *and* JOAN *enter up* L. BELMON *moves below the bed,* JACKSON *moves above the bed, and* JOAN *stands just inside the door up* L.)

BELMON (*as he enters*). Where is my Ermyntrude, where is my Ermyntrude? (*He pulls back the covers from the bed. To* LADY GEVIPHIE.) Who the hell are you?

LADY GEVIPHIE. Archie—Archibald. You've come from the dim past.

BELMON. No, madam. I've come from a warm bed.

(JACKSON *takes hold of* LADY GEVIPHIE'S *left wrist and feels her pulse.*)

JACKSON. Take it easy, my dear lady. Take it easy.

(LADY GEVIPHIE *snatches her hand away.*)

JOAN (*moving quickly to the foot of the bed*). Uncle, that's Freddie's aunt.

LADY GEVIPHIE (*reviving at the sight of* JOAN). So it's you, you brazen little thing. (*She sits up.*)

BELMON. What's this?

JACKSON. Madam, you need a sedative.

LADY GEVIPHIE. Sedative, my foot. That girl's after my nephew.

BELMON. Nonsense, my niece doesn't even know your nephew.

LADY GEVIPHIE (*moving herself out of the bed and sitting on the downstage edge of it*). Indeed. Then how is it she was undressed with him in his room?

BELMON. Undressed? Joan, deny this.

(BABA *enters* L.)

JOAN (*turning and running to* BABA). Oh, where's Freddie—he can explain. Oh, Baba, where's Mr Freddie?

BABA. I don't know, miss—he's not here.

LADY GEVIPHIE (*rising*). Good. I warned him against you, my dear—you won't see him again.

JOAN. What?

(JACKSON *moves to* JOAN *and silently comforts her.*)

BELMON (*breaking down* R.). This is beyond me.

(BABA *eases up* C., *then crosses* L. *to the dressing-table.*)

LADY GEVIPHIE. You always were a blind fool, Archibald. (*She moves to* BELMON.) You can't recognize a designing hussy today, any more than you could recognize someone who loved you in the past.

BELMON (*turning to* LADY GEVIPHIE). That voice—that face—Tiny.

LADY GEVIPHIE (*very coyly*). Yes, Archie—Tiny.

BELMON. Why, the last time I saw you I was pushing you from behind, over that orchard wall.

BABA. Ah. You wouldn't know the old place now, sir.

LADY GEVIPHIE (*moving and sitting on the luggage rack*). Ramshead.

BABA (*moving down* C.). I mean, the trees have grown since then.

BELMON. And now, Mr Ramsbottom . . .

BABA. Ramshead, to you, sir.

BELMON. What have you done with my Ermyntrude ? If she's damaged, you and Cavendish shall answer for it.

BABA. Calm yourself, sir, calm yourself. She's here, intact, and unharmed. (*He moves to the door* L. *and calls off.*) Ermyntrude—walk.

(FREDDIE, *disguised as the* ROBOT, *enters* L.)

Left.

(FREDDIE *faces the audience.*)

Stop.

(FREDDIE *stops.*)

BELMON. Oh, thank Heaven. I am relieved. If Cavendish were here I would pay him the money now instead of at the end of the week.

JOAN (*bitterly*). It's a pity he couldn't hear that. I'm sure the thought of the money would have made him stay.

BABA (*easing below* FREDDIE). Ah, miss. Many the heart the young master has broken in his mad quest for the glittering baubles of this world.

(FREDDIE *surreptitiously jabs* BABA *in the back with his knee.*)

(*He moves hurriedly* L.) Ooh !
JOAN. What's the matter ?
BABA. My old wound has broken out afresh.
JOAN. I suppose that I ought to be glad that I found out so soon.
BABA. Definitely, miss.

BELMON (*moving* R. *of* FREDDIE). Now do let me see if Ermyntrude is in perfect order. (*He starts to raise* FREDDIE'S *skirt.*) I'll check her right over.

BABA (*quickly*). You leave Ermyntrude to me. (*To* FREDDIE.) Walk—left.

(FREDDIE *faces* R.)

Other left.

(FREDDIE *turns about and moves* L.)

LADY GEVIPHIE. I don't see any point in the thing at all.
BABA. Left.

(FREDDIE *faces up stage, moves up* C. *and bumps into the wardrobe.*)

JACKSON. Professor Belmon, look.
BABA. Left.

(FREDDIE *faces* R.)

BABA. Left.

(FREDDIE *moves to* JOAN, *kisses her as he passes, then moves to* LADY GEVIPHIE *and slaps her backside.*)

LADY GEVIPHIE (*to* JACKSON). How dare you? (*She smacks* JACKSON'S *face.*)
BABA (*hysterically*). Right. Right.

(FREDDIE *faces* R., *then turns and moves up* C.)
(*He loses control.*) Left.

(FREDDIE *moves above the bed.*)
Left.

(FREDDIE *walks across the bed and moves down* R.)
Left.

(FREDDIE, *almost at the footlights, faces* L. *and moves to* BABA, *who is still down* L.)
Stop.

(FREDDIE *stops, turns and faces the audience.*)
Right.
FREDDIE (*out of the corner of his mouth ; to* BABA). I've done it.
BABA (*to* FREDDIE). You blithering idiot. (*To* BELMON.) There, Professor, what a performance.
BELMON. I'm delighted. Now all that remains is for me to take her home and give her a thorough overhaul.

(FREDDIE *and* BABA *look alarmed.*)

JOAN (*moving to* FREDDIE). Yes, Uncle, I'd like to examine her, too. (*She puts her hand to* FREDDIE'S *nose and pushes it from side to side.*)
BABA (*pushing* JOAN'S *hand away*). Practically perfect.

(*The sound of ratchet noises is heard of* L.)

BELMON. What's that?
BABA. I pulled the plug—out of the bath.
BELMON. Well, I must be off. Good-bye, Tiny, we may meet again sometime—I hope.
LADY GEVIPHIE. I hardly think so, Archibald. Next time you invent something, I suggest you invent a doctor who can keep his hands to himself.
JACKSON. Madam, I protest.
BELMON. Come on, Jackson. Joan, my dear . . .
JOAN (*looking very closely at* FREDDIE). I'm ready, Uncle. (*To* BABA.) And, Baba, next time you see Mr Cavendish, will you tell him that if ever I set eyes on him again, I shall smack his face—like this. (*She smacks* FREDDIE'S *face, turns and moves up* L.)

BELMON (*alarmed*). Joan, you might have damaged Ermyntrude. (*He moves up* L.)
BABA. Oh, no, no. Don't worry, Professor, Ermyntrude can take it. (*He slaps* FREDDIE'S *face*.)
BELMON. Ermyntrude—about turn.

(FREDDIE *turns and faces up stage*.)

Walk.

(*As* FREDDIE *starts to move up* C., *the* ROBOT, *minus its dress and wig, enters* L. *and collides with him*.)

Good heavens! What is this? I never invented two.
BABA. I think Ermyntrude's found a mate, Professor.
JOAN (*moving to* FREDDIE). I think I can help you, Uncle. (*She pulls off* FREDDIE'S *wig and hands it to* BABA.)
BELMON. What is the meaning of this?
FREDDIE. I'm sorry, but we were desperate.
LADY GEVIPHIE. Are you quite mad, Freddie?
FREDDIE. No, but I just couldn't pay for a new robot, so we hoped to convince the Professor that Ermyntrude was undamaged.
BABA. Then we'd have a week to mend her in.
JOAN (*to* FREDDIE). And it nearly came off, you dear fool.

(BELMON *moves to the* ROBOT *and examines her*.)

FREDDIE. I know just how you feel.
JOAN. You don't. (*She helps* FREDDIE *to take off his dress*.)
BABA (*to* BELMON). Is she much damaged, Professor?
BELMON. I don't know yet, but what does she look like?
JOAN (*handing the dress to* BELMON). These might improve her looks. (*She takes a handkerchief from her pocket. To* FREDDIE.) Here, let me get this off. (*She rubs the black lines from* FREDDIE'S *face*.)

(BELMON *and* BABA *put the dress and the wig on the* ROBOT.)

FREDDIE. Can you forgive me?
JOAN. No, I shall hold it over you all our lives.
LADY GEVIPHIE. What was that?
FREDDIE (*elated*). D'you mean that?
BELMON. Ermyntrude. Left.

(*The* ROBOT *faces the audience*.)

Stand clear, everybody. Ermyntrude, walk.

(*The* ROBOT *moves shakily down stage*.)

Stop.

(*The* ROBOT *stops*.)

Right.

ACT III]   THE PERFECT WOMAN   71

(*The* ROBOT *turns and faces* R.)

FREDDIE. Well, Professor ?

BELMON (*moving to the* ROBOT). I don't think she's quite balanced yet, I must adjust her gyroscope. (*He bends down and gets under the back of the* ROBOT'S *dress.*)

BABA. Is that where she keeps it ?

FREDDIE. Shut up, Baba.

BABA. Well, what's he doing ?

FREDDIE (*moving to* LADY GEVIPHIE). I don't know, but I think he's taking a photograph. (*He holds* LADY GEVIPHIE'S *arm and strikes an old-fashioned pose.*) Watch the dickeybird, Auntie.

LADY GEVIPHIE (*withdrawing her arm ; impatiently*). Tcha !

BELMON (*appearing from under the dress*). I think I've had a slight shock.

FREDDIE. Nothing surprises me tonight.

(FARINI *enters up* L., *stands looking horrified, then moves down to* R. *of the* ROBOT.)

FARINI. Mr Cavendish, if this is an English wedding night, giff me Italy. Why don't you put your arms around your wife and kiss . . .

(*The* ROBOT *puts her arms tightly around* FARINI. *There is general consternation from all. They shout excitedly except* BABA, *who remains calm.*)

BABA (*to the* ROBOT). Double-de-clutch.

(*The* ROBOT *releases* FARINI.)

FREDDIE. Well played, Baba, you remembered the word.

BELMON. What's all this talk about a wedding night ?

FREDDIE. Well, you told me to treat the robot as a wife.

BELMON. But I didn't know my niece was going to be the robot.

BABA. Believe me, sir, there was no time for dalliance.

FREDDIE (*putting his arm around* JOAN). Anyway, Professor, Joan and I are engaged.

FARINI (*clasping a hand to his forehead*). Now he's engaged to his vife.

(*He moves to the door up* L. *and exits.*)

LADY GEVIPHIE. You mean you're going to settle down together ? (*She moves between* FREDDIE *and* JOAN.) My dear child, my dear boy, that alters everything.

BELMON. Engaged—nonsense. Do you think I will allow Joan to marry a man who has no more idea of how to look after a woman than you have, besides—look how you treated my poor Ermyntrude.

JOAN. Oh, but Uncle, we love each other.

LADY GEVIPHIE (*bringing* FREDDIE *and* JOAN *together, then moving to* BELMON). Archie, they *love* each other.

BELMON. *Love*—don't talk to me about love.
FREDDIE. There—you've said it. *Love*—look at Ermyntrude.

(*The* ROBOT *now starts, slowly at first, to shoot out her arms and walk about.* FREDDIE *and* LADY GEVIPHIE *jump on to the bed,* BABA *runs and puts his head inside the bedside cabinet.* BELMON *and* JACKSON *run to the wardrobe and get inside it.* JOAN *jumps on to the armchair* L.C. *The* ROBOT *gradually accelerates and moves first down* R., *turns, crosses to* L., *turns, moves up* C., *swings round* L. *of the bed, and then moves to the door up* L. *as* WINKEL, *carrying a tray with a bottle of champagne and glasses on it, enters. The* ROBOT *collides with* WINKEL, *who drops the tray and stumbles flat on his face. She then exits up* L. *A moment later there is a terrific explosion off up* L. *and* FARINI *enters, carrying the* ROBOT'S *head and one of her hands.*)

FARINI (*moving* C. *and looking around*). Mr Cavendish.

CURTAIN

FURNITURE AND PROPERTY LIST.

ACT I.

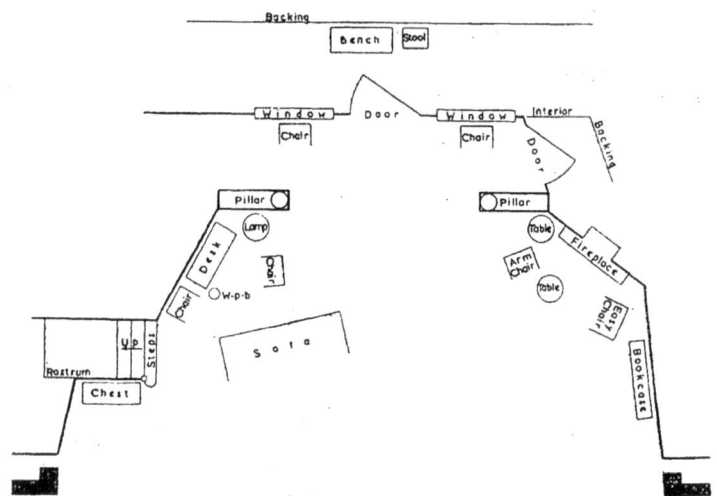

On stage.—Sofa. *On it :* cushions.
    Easy chair. *On it :* cushion.
    1 small armchair. (L.C.) *On it :* cushion.
    1 armchair. (R.)
    3 upright chairs.
    1 small table. (L.C.) *On it :* telephone, ashtray.
    1 small table (up L.) *On it :* tray, decanter of whisky, syphon of soda, box of cigarettes, table lamp, 4 glasses.
    Desk. *On it :* blotter, inkstand, pens, pair of brass candlesticks desk lamp, ashtray.
    Waste-paper basket.
    Bookcase. *In it :* books.
    Oak chest. *On it :* cushion.
    Standard lamp.
    On mantelpiece : ornaments, ashtray, lists.
    In fireplace : screen, fire-irons.
    Fender.
    Hearth rug.
    Carpet on floor.
    Carpet on stairs.
    1 pair net curtains.
    1 pair heavy curtains.
    Pictures on walls.
    4 electric wall brackets.
    In laboratory: chrome-legged table. *On it :* bottles of chemicals. Chrome-legged, leather-topped stools.
    Light switches. (R. of fireplace.)
    Bell push. (R. of door up C.)

74 THE PERFECT WOMAN

Off stage.—Newspaper. (BUDDY.)
Pair of nylons in packet. (BUDDY.)
Dress box. (GRUBB.)
Hat. (FREDDIE.)
Hat, gloves, umbrella. (BABA.)
Dummy hand. (BABA.)
Dummy leg. (FREDDIE.)
Wheel-chair and dust sheet. (FREDDIE.)

Personal.—JACKSON : Pipe, pouch, matches, watch, wallet. *In it :* ten £1 notes.
BUDDY : Lighter.
FREDDIE : Lighter.
BABA : Handkerchief.
BELMON : Wallet. *In it :* twenty £1 notes.

ACT II.

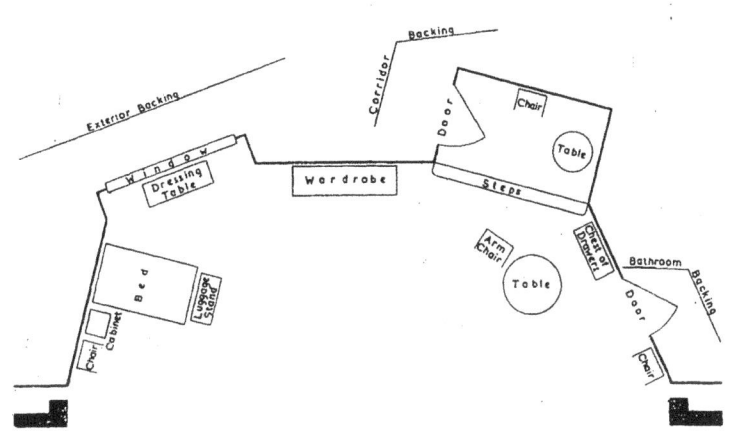

On stage.—Double bed. *On it :* mattress, sheets, blanket, silk coverlet, pillows.
Luggage rack.
Bedside cabinet. *On it :* table lamp, telephone, ashtray, telephone directory.
3 upright chairs.
Armchair.
Large circular table.
Small circular table. (In alcove.) *On it :* empty vase.
Chest of drawers. *On it :* vase of flowers, ashtray.
Wardrobe. *In it :* 3 coat hangers.
Dressing-table. *On it :* candle lamps, ashtray.
Carpet on floor.
1 pair net curtains.
1 pair heavy curtains.
4 electric wall brackets.

Light pendant.
Light switches (below door up L.)
Off stage.—Suitcase. *In it :* nail brush. (BABA).
Bunch of flowers. (WINKEL.)
Towel. (FREDDIE.)
Tray. *On it :* silver bowl of soup, ladle, 3 soup plates. (FARINI.)
Table. *On it :* cloth, 3 table napkins, 3 small plates. *On them :* bread. Cruet, 3 soup spoons, 3 knives, 3 forks, 3 glasses. (WINKEL.)
3 plates of chicken. (WINKEL.)
2 vegetable dishes. (WINKEL.)
Basket of bottles. (WINKEL.)
Personal.—FREDDIE : Lists.
LADY GEVIPHIE : Brooch.

ACT III.

Set.—Bottle on bedside cabinet.
Magazine on bed.
Off stage.—2 bottles. (WINKEL.)
Tray. *On it :* bottle of champagne, glasses. (WINKEL.)
Dummy head and hand. (FARINI.)
Personal.—BABA. Wrist watch.
LADY GEVIPHIE : Brooch.
JOAN : Handkerchief.

LIGHTING PLOT.

ACT I.

To open : Laboratory light—on.
Table lamp—on.
Wall bracket over stairs—on.
Cue 1 : GRUBB switches on lights. All lights up to full.
Cue 2 : BELMON switches off laboratory light.
Cue 3 : BELMON switches on laboratory light.
Cue 4 : BELMON switches off laboratory light.
Cue 5 : FREDDIE switches on laboratory light.
This lighting stands until the end of the Act.

ACT II.

To open : Stage in darkness.
Light behind door up L.—on.
Cue 1 : FARINI switches on lights. Pendant, wall brackets, dressing-table lights—on.
Cue 2 : FARINI switches on light in bathroom.
Cue 3 : FARINI switches on bedside lamp. All lights up to full.
This lighting stands until the end of the Act.

ACT III.

To open : Lights dimmed to ¼. Bedside lamp—on.
Cue 1 : LADY GEVIPHIE switches on lights. All lights up to full. Pendant, wall brackets, dressing-table lights—on.
Cue 2 : BABA switches off bedside lamp. Lights down to ¾.
Cue 3 : BABA switches off lights. Stage lights black-out.
Cue 4 : BABA switches on bedside lamp. Lights up to ¼.
Cue 5 : FREDDIE switches on lights. All lights up to full.
Cue 6 : Flash of light off up L. at explosion.

www.ingramcontent.com/pod-product-compliance
Ingram Content Group UK Ltd.
Pitfield, Milton Keynes, MK11 3LW, UK
UKHW021837210426
53221PUK00021B/333